AF784689

CONTENTS

GETTING BETTER VALUE IN HEALTH CARE

HEARING

BEFORE THE

COMMITTEE ON THE BUDGET
HOUSE OF REPRESENTATIVES

ONE HUNDRED TENTH CONGRESS

SECOND SESSION

HEARING HELD IN WASHINGTON, DC, JULY 16, 2008

Serial No. 110–37

Printed for the use of the Committee on the Budget

Available on the Internet:
http://www.gpoaccess.gov/congress/house/budget/index.html

U.S. GOVERNMENT PRINTING OFFICE

44–037 PDF WASHINGTON : 2008

For sale by the Superintendent of Documents, U.S. Government Printing Office
Internet: bookstore.gpo.gov Phone: toll free (866) 512–1800; DC area (202) 512–1800
Fax: (202) 512–2104 Mail: Stop IDCC, Washington, DC 20402–0001

COMMITTEE ON THE BUDGET

JOHN M. SPRATT, Jr., South Carolina, *Chairman*

ROSA L. DeLAURO, Connecticut,
CHET EDWARDS, Texas
JIM COOPER, Tennessee
THOMAS H. ALLEN, Maine
ALLYSON Y. SCHWARTZ, Pennsylvania
MARCY KAPTUR, Ohio
XAVIER BECERRA, California
LLOYD DOGGETT, Texas
EARL BLUMENAUER, Oregon
MARION BERRY, Arkansas
ALLEN BOYD, Florida
JAMES P. McGOVERN, Massachusetts
NIKI TSONGAS, Massachusetts
ROBERT E. ANDREWS, New Jersey
ROBERT C. "BOBBY" SCOTT, Virginia
BOB ETHERIDGE, North Carolina
DARLENE HOOLEY, Oregon
BRIAN BAIRD, Washington
DENNIS MOORE, Kansas
TIMOTHY H. BISHOP, New York
GWEN MOORE, Wisconsin

PAUL RYAN, Wisconsin,
Ranking Minority Member
J. GRESHAM BARRETT, South Carolina
JO BONNER, Alabama
SCOTT GARRETT, New Jersey
MARIO DIAZ-BALART, Florida
JEB HENSARLING, Texas
DANIEL E. LUNGREN, California
MICHAEL K. SIMPSON, Idaho
PATRICK T. McHENRY, North Carolina
CONNIE MACK, Florida
K. MICHAEL CONAWAY, Texas
JOHN CAMPBELL, California
PATRICK J. TIBERI, Ohio
JON C. PORTER, Nevada
RODNEY ALEXANDER, Louisiana
ADRIAN SMITH, Nebraska
JIM JORDAN, Ohio

Professional Staff

Thomas S. Kahn, *Staff Director and Chief Counsel*
Austin Smythe, *Minority Staff Director*

GETTING BETTER VALUE IN HEALTH CARE

WEDNESDAY, JULY 16, 2008

HOUSE OF REPRESENTATIVES,
COMMITTEE ON THE BUDGET,
Washington, DC.

The committee met, pursuant to call, at 10:10 a.m., in Room 210, Cannon House Office Building, Hon. John Spratt [chairman of the committee] presiding.

Present: Representatives Spratt, Schwartz, Kaptur, Becerra, Doggett, Berry, Scott, Etheridge, Moore of Kansas, Ryan, Conaway, Alexander, and Smith.

Chairman SPRATT. I call the hearing to order.

Good morning and welcome to the House Budget Committee's hearing on Getting Better Value Out of Health Care. We have three outstanding witnesses with us today to help us understand what needs to be done to ensure that our money is spent wisely and well on health care both in the private and public sectors.

CBO's Director Peter Orszag has made a great contribution towards helping us in Congress understand better the issues and levers that are available to us in the arena of health care. I can't understate how much we appreciate his advice and input.

Jeanne Lambrew is a health policy expert now at the University of Texas, a constituent of Lloyd Doggett, but we know her from years past for her excellent advice and participation in these issues as well.

Dr. David Gratzer is a physician who has practiced in Canada and the United States, which gives him a special perspective to bring to the table today. I thank all three witnesses for coming and we look forward to your testimony.

Health care spending has outpaced U.S. economic growth for quite some time and, frankly, is expected to continue doing so. This overall trend has significant implications for our Federal budget. CBO projects its spending for Medicare and Medicaid under current law could more than quadruple as a percent of GDP over the next 75 years, growing from 4.1 percent of GDP today to 18.6 percent of GDP by 2082. CBO also projects that based on current trends and policy preferences, the gap between Federal spending and revenues over the next 75 years is 6.9 percent of GDP.

To address this long-term fiscal imbalance, everything will have to be on the table and everyone will have to be at the table, but it is also clear that these budget decisions cannot be made in a vacuum. Putting the budget on a sustainable path inescapably involves the need to address the growth trends in overall health care spending.

We have held a number of hearings on this subject, and we will hold more. Today's hearing gives us a chance to delve a bit deeper into some of the challenges and opportunities in health care.

We do not know with any certainty today how much society can or should spend for the health care we all desire, but we do know it makes no sense to spend money on health care that is ineffective or potentially even harmful to patients.

Dr. Orszag has noted in previous testimony that there are significant opportunities to reduce health care costs without harming health care outcomes. It is critical that we begin to explore these opportunities, especially in connection with a system-wide look at both public and private health care. Today's hearing gives us just that opportunity.

Before turning to our witnesses for their testimony, let me go to Ranking Member Ryan and ask him for any opening statement he would like to make.

Mr. Ryan.

Mr. RYAN. Thank you, Mr. Chairman. As usual, another great hearing. A very timely topic and fantastic witnesses.

Access to quality, affordable medical care is critically important to all Americans, and that is why this hearing is so timely. The problem is, we are spending more than $2 trillion a year on health care, and that number continues to skyrocket. But we still have 47 million people without health insurance, and many others are afraid they might lose their coverage because costs are rising too fast for them to keep up with it.

We can and we must get control of health care costs, and there are a number of steps we can make to improve this situation, some of which we are going to be discussing here today. But we need to be sure that we start in the right place, and that would be the argument I would make.

The real cornerstone of health care is the relationship between the individual patient and their doctor. So whatever we do, we ought to aim to strengthen and reinforce that relationship.

We can achieve that goal by removing the distortions in the health care marketplace to make it more competitive and more cost-effective. That was one of the guiding principles in the health care component of a plan I introduced in May that I call a Roadmap for America's Future. I believe that some of the elements of my plan will be consistent with some of the recommendations of our witnesses here today, so I will briefly just note a few.

First, we need to recognize that the current third-party payment arrangements promoted by the Federal tax exclusion for employer-based health insurance and by the structure of Medicare and Medicaid themselves remove patients from the decision-making process and hide the true costs of services. The tax treatment also discriminates against workers and families who do not have employer-sponsored health insurance.

Placing the tax benefit in the hands of individuals and families will lead to better competition, which will spur greater options and higher-quality services to meet the diverse needs of Americans, just as it does in all the other sectors of the U.S. economy.

Second, making price and quality data available to everyone is critical. It is critical to the success of an effective health care marketplace. Individuals and families must have a better sense of what they are expected to pay for health care and what they are going to get for their money.

Third, just as individuals ought to be able to own their own health care coverage, they should also own their own health care records. This can be done by making medical records electronic and portable.

Finally, we have got to recognize that we will never get ahold of overall medical costs without also addressing the structure of Federal health entitlements. We know this all too well on this committee. Medicare and Medicaid make up one-third of all health care spending nationally, so clearly this has a huge impact on the overall health care financing network.

As I said at the start, because Americans want quality, affordable medical care, we will always spend a large share of our economic resources to get it. But we can certainly get more value for what we spend today, and I look forward to hearing from our witnesses on how we just do that on this critical issue.

Thank you, Mr. Chairman.

Chairman SPRATT. I ask unanimous consent that all members be allowed, if they wish, to submit an opening statement for the record at this point.

Without objection, so ordered.

[The prepared statement of Mr. Smith follows:]

PREPARED STATEMENT OF HON. ADRIAN SMITH, A REPRESENTATIVE IN CONGRESS FROM THE STATE OF NEBRASKA

Good morning. Thank you, Mr. Chairman, for convening this hearing today on Getting Better Value in Health Care. Thank you also to our distinguished panel of witnesses.

With Medicare, Medicaid, and Social Security consuming 8.4% of the federal budget, and expected to grow to 18.9% by 2050, we cannot hope to balance the budget if we do not find ways to encourage more efficient use of health care dollars. Collecting and sharing data on the effectiveness of various treatments is one way we could encourage better decisions. By doing so, we would be able to demonstrate to both providers and patients the most common or expensive course of treatment is not always the most effective, and begin encouraging better use of Medicare's limited funds.

We must remember, however, that doctors and patients, not politicians, are best equipped to determine the proper course of treatment. While comparative effectiveness data can be a useful tool in saving lives and money, patients have unique needs, and this information should not be used to mandate treatment for anyone. Not only do patients react differently to treatment, but often the best course of treatment for seniors in large cities with ready access to health care facilities may not be right for a senior in rural Nebraska who must travel 50 to 100 miles or more round trip to see a specialist for the same condition.

We must remember comparative effectiveness is not a panacea. We must also pursue any number of other solutions to encourage the smart, efficient use of health care dollars if Medicare is going to be around for our children and grandchildren.

Thank you again, Mr. Chairman and panelists. I am looking forward to learning much more this morning about how we can more efficiently provide health care to our seniors.

Chairman SPRATT. Let's begin our witnesses today with Dr. Orszag.

Dr. Orszag and all of our witnesses, you should be on notice that your entire statement will be made part of the record so that you can summarize it as you see fit. But the floor is yours to take as much time as you need to explain your points today.

Let's begin, as I said, with Dr. Orszag.

Thank you, sir, for coming. We look forward to your testimony.

STATEMENT OF PETER ORSZAG, DIRECTOR, CONGRESSIONAL BUDGET OFFICE

Mr. ORSZAG. Thank you, Mr. Spratt, Mr. Ryan, members of the committee.

Health care contains, in my opinion, the largest inefficiencies in our economy. Credible estimates suggest that as much as $700 billion a year in health care services delivered do not improve health outcomes. That is 5 percent of our national income. There is no other inefficiency that I can identify that comes close to it.

Health care costs are also the key to our fiscal future, as the first chart shows—or is about to show—with very rapid growth in Medicare and Medicaid being the dominant force in spending over the long term.

It is also the case, as an illustration of the inefficiencies that I mentioned, that health care costs vary quite substantially across different parts of the United States, as the second chart shows, for reasons that cannot be explained based on the severity of illnesses in different parts of the country or the prices of building a hospital or paying a doctor in different parts of the country. And the darker blue areas of the country—I should probably say that sometimes this graph is presented in red and sometimes in blue; today it is blue. The darker blue parts of the country have significantly higher costs mostly because of more intensive treatment patterns—not because things cost more there, but rather because there is more done there.

The interesting part is as you look at the next chart, there is no additional benefit that you seem to get from the higher spending areas. So the higher spending is not associated with better health outcomes or higher quality than lower spending areas. And we see that even at our leading medical centers, where there are significant variations in the cost of treating a patient across our top medical centers that don't correlate or do not seem to generate improvements in health outcomes. I think that is perhaps the most telling illustration of this significant inefficiency.

So what do we do about it? It seems to me like there are three steps that are crucial to any plan to attack this problem.

The first is, we need much more information on what works and what doesn't. Far too much of the medical care delivered in the United States is not backed by specific evidence that it works better than anything else, and much of that additional intensity in the higher spending regions is of low or zero value apparent care, again because it is not backed by any specific evidence that it works better.

In order to get that information on what works and what doesn't, we likely will need a more universal system of health information technology. And I would just immediately say if you were serious about getting there, rather than providing small subsidies for hospitals and doctors to adopt health information technology, which would only affect those entities that were close to adopting voluntarily, you could very quickly get to nearly universal health information technology if you said to hospitals and doctors, you have 3 or 4 years to adopt a health IT system that meets the following qualifications, and after that you won't be reimbursed under Medicare unless you have such a system in place.

If you did that, I am very certain we would have nearly universal health IT very quickly.

In addition, you need some system for using the information and evaluating what is coming out of the health IT system through some sort of comparative effectiveness research entity or entities. So that is more information.

Secondly, we need to change the incentives in health care. Right now we have financial incentives for more care rather than better care, and we are not going to get better care unless we create incentives for that. What that means is basically paying more for the stuff that works and not paying for or paying less for the stuff that doesn't. We can talk more about that.

I also think we need to be doing a lot more on healthy living and helping people live the kinds of lives that most people say they want to. On that point, I would say I feel like I was mistrained as an economist, and we are learning from behavioral economics and psychology that a lot of personal behavior is driven by social norms, by the way things are presented, by what the default is, what happens automatically, and that financial incentives can matter, but they matter often much less than those other things. So the purely rational Economics 101 perspective, which is at the heart of a lot of public policy, is very limited in terms of how effective it is in affecting personal behavior.

I would just close by noting, I think one of the significant impediments that we face is a political economy one, which is that most workers don't seem to appreciate how much health care costs are actually bearing on them because the costs are hidden in the form of employer contributions for health insurance; and even though all of the evidence suggests that workers do bear those costs through reduced take-home pay, it is not salient. People don't focus on that, and most people I think don't recognize how much the system is actually costing us.

Secondly, there are questions about whether our political system deals well with gradual, long-term problems like this one, gradually increasing costs. On that point, I would note there may be process changes that could help. There have been ideas floated for a Federal health board, which we could discuss in more detail. And also, unlike some other long-term challenges that we face, this one has things that are happening today. As I have already said, workers' wages are being reduced to a degree that perhaps is underappreciated and unnecessarily large.

At the State level, Medicaid costs are crowding out State support for higher education and thereby raising public tuition today. And your taxpayer dollars are financing care at UCLA Medical for Medicare beneficiaries in the last 6 months of life that cost an average of $50,000 a year, and at the Mayo Clinic for Medicare beneficiaries in the last 6 months of life $26,000 a year; and I cannot tell you what we are getting in exchange for the extra money.

Thank you very much, Mr. Chairman.

Chairman SPRATT. Thank you, Dr. Orszag.

[The prepared statement of Peter Orszag follows:]

Congressional Budget Office

Testimony

Statement of
Peter R. Orszag
Director

Increasing the Value of Federal Spending on Health Care

before the
Committee on the Budget
U.S. House of Representatives

July 16, 2008

This document is embargoed until it is delivered at 10:00 a.m. (EDT) on Wednesday, July 16, 2008. The contents may not be published, transmitted, or otherwise communicated by any print, broadcast, or electronic media before that time.

CONGRESSIONAL BUDGET OFFICE
SECOND AND D STREETS, S.W.
WASHINGTON, D.C. 20515

NOTE.—This statement reprises a presentation given at the Senate Finance Committee's "Health Reform Summit," in Washington, DC, on June 6, 2008.

Chairman Spratt, Ranking Member Ryan, and Members of the Committee, thank you for giving me the opportunity to discuss opportunities for increasing the efficiency of health care. The rate of growth in health care costs is the most important factor influencing the federal government's long-term fiscal situation. The Congressional Budget Office (CBO) projects that, without any changes in federal law, total spending on health care will rise from 16 percent of the gross domestic product (GDP) in 2007 to 25 percent in 2025 and 49 percent in 2082, and net federal spending on Medicare and Medicaid will rise from 4 percent of GDP to almost 20 percent over the same period.[1] Many of the other factors that will play a key role in determining future fiscal conditions—including the actuarial deficit in Social Security and a decision about extending the 2001 and 2003 tax legislation past its scheduled expiration in 2010—pale by comparison over the long term with the impact and challenges of containing growth in the cost of federal health insurance programs.

Both demographic changes and rising health care costs per beneficiary contribute significantly to our future fiscal challenges, but it seems clear that the latter is more important over the long term. To be sure, among adults, health care spending generally increases with age. As the number of elderly people increases over time, health care spending naturally will grow. Yet the dominance of cost growth in health care over the effect of demographic changes can be seen by comparing the trajectory of cost growth in Social Security with that in Medicare and Medicaid over time (see Figure 1).

Given the nature of the programs, a demographic shift will have similar effects on the costs of Social Security and of Medicare and Medicaid. In the next 10 to 20 years, the projected growth of spending in those programs differs but perhaps not all that dramatically, which suggests that demographics account for a relatively large share of the increase during that period. Beyond that point, however, Social Security spending levels off as a share of GDP, while spending on Medicare and Medicaid is projected to grow much more rapidly. Some have interpreted that relative dominance of cost growth per beneficiary in influencing our fiscal future as an excuse for not addressing the higher costs associated with an aging population. That reasoning makes little sense to me; it is a non sequitur. To say that problem A is bigger than problem B is not to say that problem B does not exist or should not be addressed.

My statement briefly explores evidence of the potentially substantial inefficiencies in health care and then discusses a few pathways to reducing them.

Evidence of Inefficiency

Embedded in the nation's long-term fiscal challenge is a substantial opportunity: to reduce health care costs without adversely affecting health outcomes. Perhaps the

1. Congressional Budget Office, *The Long-Term Outlook for Health Care Spending* (November 2007).

Figure 1.

Federal Spending Under CBO's Alternative Fiscal Scenario

(Percentage of gross domestic product)

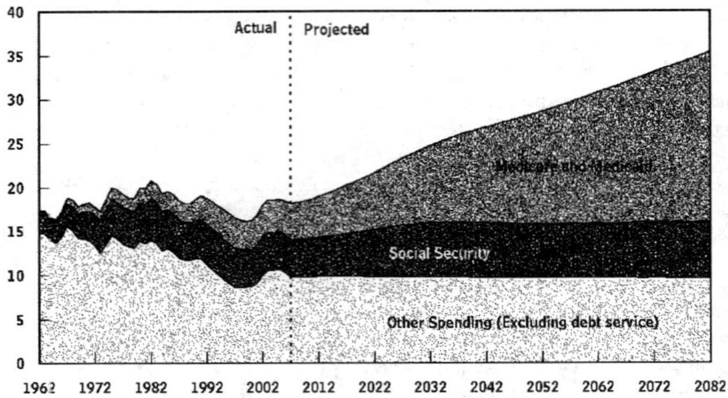

Source: Congressional Budget Office.

most compelling evidence suggesting that opportunity is that per capita health care spending varies widely across the United States (see Figure 2), and yet the very substantial variation in cost per beneficiary is not correlated with health outcomes overall. For example, a comparison of composite quality scores for medical centers, on the one hand, and average spending per beneficiary, on the other, shows that facilities in states with high average costs are no more likely to provide recommended care for some common health problems than are facilities in states with lower costs (see Figure 3); if anything, it would appear that the opposite might be true.

Variations in health care are often most dramatic when there is uncertainty about what kind of treatment to administer. For example, it is clear that aspirin should almost always be provided to a patient upon admission to the hospital for a heart attack, and there is very little variation in that practice. However, there is significant geographic variation in the use of imaging and diagnostic tests, and it is often unclear when those services generate useful information or how frequently they should be provided.

Similarly, admission to the hospital for a hip fracture is always indicated, and admission rates for people with that injury show little variation; but much less of a consensus exists about back surgery, and the related admission rates vary much more widely. Overuse of supply-sensitive services and differences in social norms among local physicians seem to drive regional approaches in the use of innovations and treatments. Some regions appear more prone to adopt low-cost, highly effective patterns of care,

Figure 2.

Medicare Spending per Beneficiary in the United States, by Hospital Referral Region, 2005

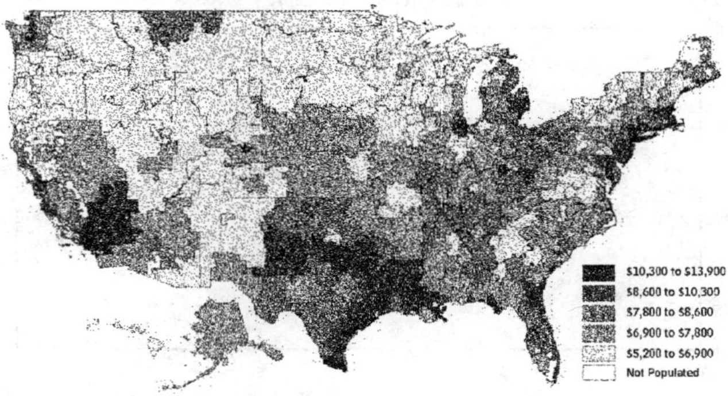

Source: Congressional Budget Office based on data from the Centers for Medicare and Medicaid Services.

Note: The data are for Medicare spending per beneficiary in the fee-for-service program, adjusted for age, sex, and race. The geographic unit is the hospital referral region, as defined by the Dartmouth Atlas of Health Care. Areas labeled "Not Populated" include places such as national parks, forests, lakes, and islands.

whereas others are more prone to adopt high-cost patterns of care and to deliver treatments that provide little benefit or are even harmful.

One might note that some of the highest-cost areas are concentrated around the top U.S. medical centers and assume that it is the work of those centers that drives the cost differences across the nation. However, even among elite medical centers, there is significant variation in cost. Among the UCLA (University of California, Los Angeles) Medical Center, Massachusetts General Hospital, and the Mayo Clinic (St. Mary's Hospital), for example, composite quality scores are very similar (81.5, 85.9, and 90.4, respectively). Although the Mayo Clinic scores above the other two, its cost per beneficiary for Medicare clients in the last six months of life ($26,330) is nearly half that at the UCLA Medical Center ($50,522) and significantly lower than the cost at Massachusetts General Hospital ($40,181). Uwe Reinhardt, renowned professor of economics at Princeton University, asks, "How can it be that 'the best medical care in the world' costs twice as much as the best medical care in the world?"[2]

2. As quoted in Gina Kolata, "Sharp Regional Incongruity Found in Medical Costs and Treatments," *Women's Health*, January 30, 1996, available at www.nytimes.com/specials/women/warchive/960130_1576.html.

Figure 3.

The Relationship Between Quality of Care and Medicare Spending, by State, 2004

(Composite measure of quality of care, 100 = maximum)

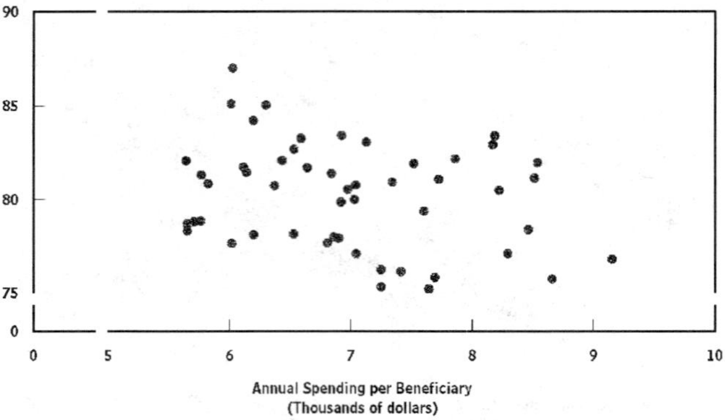

Source: Congressional Budget Office based on data from the Centers for Medicare and Medicaid Services and from Department of Health and Human Services, Agency for Healthcare Research and Quality, *National Healthcare Quality Report, 2005* (December 2005), Data Tables Appendix, available at www.ahrq.gov/qual/nhqr05/index.html.

Notes: The composite measure of the quality of care, based on Medicare beneficiaries in the fee-for-service program who were hospitalized in 2004, conveys the percentage who received recommended care for myocardial infarction, heart failure, or pneumonia.

Spending figures convey average amounts by state.

So how much could all this amount to? Researchers have estimated that nearly 30 percent of Medicare's costs could be saved without negatively affecting health outcomes if spending in high- and medium-cost areas could be reduced to the level in low-cost areas—and those estimates could probably be extrapolated to the health care system as a whole.[3] With health care spending currently representing 16 percent of GDP, that estimate would suggest that nearly 5 percent of GDP—or roughly $700 billion each year—goes to health care spending that cannot be shown to improve health outcomes. Of course, figuring out how to reduce spending only for inappropriate and unnecessary care is a not a trivial exercise. Nevertheless, there do not appear to be other examples that credible analysts can identify that offer a potential efficiency gain of that magnitude for the U.S. economy.

3. John E. Wennberg and others, "Geography and the Debate Over Medicare Reform," *Health Affairs*, Web Exclusive (February 13, 2002), pp. W96–W114; and Elliott Fisher, "More Care Is Not Better Care," *Expert Voices*, Issue 7 (National Institute for Health Care Management, January 2005).

The idea that there could be such a potentially large inefficiency—valued at $700 billion per year—in the health care system is striking. Also striking is the relatively small investment in research focused on the mechanics of restructuring the delivery of and payments for health care to reduce inefficiency.

Behavioral Economics and Efficiency in the Health Sector

One factor helping to perpetuate inefficiencies in health care is a lack of clarity regarding what insurance costs and who bears those costs, especially for employment-based health insurance. Employers' payments for employment-based health insurance and nearly all payments by employees for that insurance are excluded from individual income and payroll taxes. Although both theory and evidence suggest that workers ultimately finance their employment-based insurance through lower take-home pay, the costs are not evident to many workers.

We know from other settings that salience matters—and indeed that it often matters much more than the underlying financial incentives, at least when relatively small sums are involved. When consumers go into a store, for example, they see pretax prices on the items. One might assume—or at least the Econ 101 rational optimizing model would assume—that consumers are generally aware of which items are taxable and what the tax rate is. But studies in the growing field of behavioral economics question such assumptions. For example, when researchers went into a grocery store and posted after-tax prices on some items, sales of those goods fell by about 8 percent.[4] They found similar effects when examining the effects of sales taxes and excise taxes (which are included in posted prices) on alcohol sales. Another study looked at a related question: When highway tolls are automated, does the reduced salience induce higher prices?[5] The answer is that it does. The author found that toll rates were 20 percent to 40 percent higher than they would have been without electronic toll collection.

I suspect, on the basis of similar logic, that workers demand less efficiency from the health system than they would if they knew the full cost that they pay via forgone wages for coverage. I suspect also that making the underlying costs associated with employment-based insurance more transparent might prove to be quite important in containing health care costs. For workers and dependents with employment-based insurance, deductibles and copayments account for only about a fifth of their health care spending. The remainder comes from insurance premiums, only a quarter of which is paid directly by workers. As transparency increases and workers see how much their income is being reduced for employers' contributions and what those con-

4. Raj Chetty, Adam Looney, and Kory Kroft, *Salience and Taxation: Theory and Evidence*, Working Paper No. 13330 (Cambridge, Mass.: National Bureau of Economic Research, August 2007).

5. Amy Finkelstein, *E-ZTax: Tax Salience and Tax Rates*, Working Paper No. 12924 (Cambridge, Mass.: National Bureau of Economic Research, January 2007).

tributions are paying for, there might be a broader change in cost-consciousness that shifts demand.

Pathways to Improving Efficiency

What could be done to improve the efficiency with which health care is delivered—and specifically to reduce the delivery of services with little or no value? In health care, the vast majority of decisions are heavily influenced by doctors and other medical professionals. Restraining cost growth will therefore primarily require changing their choices. Cost constraints could be implemented by refusing to pay for certain services; I suspect, however, that more subtle actions may be more sustainable.

Like other people, doctors tend to follow professional norms of behavior. There are a number of reasons for that behavior, among them that following professional norms is simple and that it may help defend against charges of malpractice. The problem is that the professional norms in different parts of the nation do not always follow evidence-based standards of best practice. Indeed, the regional pattern of health care delivery (apparent in Figure 2) probably reflects, at least in part, differences in norms of practice among doctors. Professional norms may differ by locality because local colleagues may have a disproportionate influence and because bias favoring the status quo may make norms slow to change in the face of new evidence.

How can norms be shifted? Two potentially complementary approaches to reducing total health care spending involve generating more information about the relative effectiveness of medical treatments and changing the incentives for providers and consumers of health care. More information on the "comparative effectiveness" of alternative medical treatments could offer a basis for ensuring that future technologies and existing costly services are used only in cases in which they confer clinical benefits that are superior to those of other, cheaper services. Analysis of comparative effectiveness is simply a comparison of the impact of different options that are available for treating a given medical condition in a particular set of patients.

Anesthesiology provides one example of a great success story in putting evidence-based standards into practice. In the mid-1980s, after analyzing the most common sources of errors, the American Society of Anesthesiologists promulgated standards of optimal practice (both in procedures and equipment).[6] Providers had an incentive to follow the standards because deviations from them made the imposition of malpractice liability more likely. After the standards were adopted, mortality rates fell to about 5 per million encounters, as compared with averages above 100 per million during

6. See Jeffrey B. Cooper, "Getting Into Patient Safety: A Personal Story," *AHRQ WebM&M: Morbidity and Mortality Rounds on the Web* (Agency for Healthcare Research and Quality, August 2006), available at www.webmm.ahrq.gov/perspective.aspx?perspectiveID=29.

earlier periods.[7] Thus, aggressively promulgated standards backed by some incentives can alter a long-standing and suboptimal status quo.

Research suggests, however, that the merely providing information to physicians results in an "exceedingly modest behavioral response."[8] The current financial incentives for both providers and patients tend to encourage or at least facilitate the adoption of expensive treatments and procedures, even if evidence about their effectiveness relative to existing therapies is limited. Costly services that are known to be highly effective for some patients are sometimes provided to others for whom the clinical benefits have not been rigorously demonstrated. Therefore, to alter providers' behavior, it is probably necessary to combine comparative effectiveness research with aggressive promulgation of standards and changes in financial and other incentives.[9]

Inefficiency and Price Transparency for Specific Medical Services

Let me also address the effect of transparency with regard to specific medical services. Some observers believe that if people know the prices of health care services, they are more likely to seek out less expensive providers or treatments and to question how effective the care they are purchasing is likely to be. But several factors may limit the effectiveness of that type of transparency in cutting health care expenditures.

On the consumer side, more than 80 percent of the population is covered by some form of health insurance, which insulates people from the full price of their health care, limiting their incentive to compare prices. Doctors and other health professionals often direct the decisions about what services to buy from whom, as patients may have little information on the care they need or the quality or value of that care. Moreover, for insured and uninsured people alike, awareness of prices will make little difference in emergencies or in the relatively small number of cases that account for a disproportionate share of overall health care spending.

On the provider side, more transparency would make information about the prices that hospitals, physicians, and drug companies charge insurers more visible, but whether such disclosure would lead to higher or lower prices for consumers on average is unclear and depends on the nature of competition in the relevant market. The markets for some health care services are highly concentrated, so increasing transparency in such markets could lead to higher, rather than lower, prices because higher prices are easier to maintain when the prices charged by each provider involved can be

7. See David Hyman and Charles Silver, "You Get What You Pay For: Result-Based Compensation for Health Care," *Washington and Lee Law Review* (Fall 2001).

8. David E. Kanouse, Joel Kallich, and James P. Kahan. "Dissemination of Effectiveness and Outcomes Research," *Health Policy*, vol. 34, no. 3 (1995), pp. 167–192.

9. See Congressional Budget Office, *Research on the Comparative Effectiveness of Medical Treatments: Issues and Options for an Expanded Federal Role* (December 2007).

observed by all of the others. However, aggregated information or information on average prices would make it more difficult for providers to coordinate higher prices because individual providers' prices would not be obvious. Whatever the effect on average prices, more transparent prices would probably reduce the range of prices.[10]

CBO's Activities

Because future health care spending is the single most important factor determining the nation's long-term fiscal condition, CBO is devoting increasing resources to assessing options for reducing such spending in the future. The agency has expanded the number of full-time-equivalent staff analyzing health care issues from 30 at roughly this time last year to 45 now, with 3 more coming on board within the next three months. Last year, CBO established a panel of health advisers (consisting of experts from academia, industry, and independent research organizations), which meets periodically to examine frontier research in health policy and to advise the agency on its analyses of health care issues. As part of its work generally, CBO continually reviews research conducted both in and outside of government. Late this year, the agency plans to release two reports on health policy: One will present budget estimates for numerous specific policy options, and the other will address critical topics related to proposals to make major changes in the health care system. CBO hopes that those efforts will be of significant value to the Congress in assessing ways to address these critical policy issues.

10. See Congressional Budget Office, *Increasing Transparency in the Pricing of Health Care Services and Pharmaceuticals* (June 5, 2008).

Chairman SPRATT. Now Dr. Lambrew.

STATEMENT OF JEANNE M. LAMBREW, PH.D., ASSOCIATE PROFESSOR, LYNDON B. JOHNSON SCHOOL OF PUBLIC AFFAIRS, UNIVERSITY OF TEXAS AT AUSTIN, AND SENIOR FELLOW, CENTER FOR AMERICAN PROGRESS ACTION FUND

Ms. LAMBREW. Thank you, Chairman Spratt, Ranking Member Ryan and distinguished members of the committee. I thank you for the opportunity to testify on the topic of value in health care. Arguably, few other topics are more important to your work.

As Dr. Orszag just laid out, the long-run budget problems are largely driven by health care cost growth, and fiscal stability cannot be achieved without health reform. As such, it is both a health priority as well as a budget priority. In my testimony, I suggest how value in the care system can be enhanced and why the opportunity for doing so is on the horizon.

To begin with, health care is complex, eluding simple rules. Technological advances in medicine tend to increase the need for high-paid specialists rather than improving productivity. Providers determine demand, as well as meet it, insurers have little incentive to promote value when enrollees come and go, and people believe that high-cost care equals high-quality care, despite evidence to the contrary. As such, no single simple plan can achieve value. Instead, I suggest that it requires an adaptable infrastructure through which changing information, best practices and incentives for use can be channeled.

The first component of such an infrastructure is standards. Despite evidence on the benefits and trade-offs for many treatments, no authoritative synthesis of such information exists. Instead, different and sometimes conflicting standards are used across the Nation. This has resulted in low use of recommended care, high use of questionable care, and unnecessary complexity for doctors and patients. Creating a standard-setting process to guide health care decisions could improve value in the health care system.

Second, dissemination is as critical as the development of these standards. Standards can only affect performance if they reach the remote parts of our health care system and vice versa. Information and expertise from all parts of the health care system are needed to set standards. Information networks can accelerate access to best practices and provide data to inform them.

Third, knowledge is necessary, but not sufficient. Financial incentives for providers and patients should be steered towards value, not just costs. Public subsidies of private insurers could also leverage value-based coverage, and the delivery system itself could be redesigned to make high-value health care in coverage the easiest choice for individuals and providers.

Such infrastructure to promote standards through dissemination and their use can undergird a number of different health reform proposals, although their efficacy is maximized in a seamless system with sustainable financing. In my testimony, I have described five policies that could lay the groundwork for value oriented health care. Here I list three.

The first, echoing what Dr. Orszag just said, is investing in comparative effectiveness research. A prerequisite to assigning value is knowing the relative impact of the various health services and delivery modes. So-called comparative effectiveness research has support from a wide range of businesses, consumer groups and experts.

Bipartisan legislation has been introduced, and the Congressional Budget Office estimated that that proposal could save the system up to $6 billion over 10 years. Congress should enact this legislation, since this information is the building block for a value-based system.

Second, policymakers could create a Federal Reserve-like board to set standards. This board would be an authoritative source of information on the value and trade-offs associated with health care services and delivery mechanisms. It could focus on high-cost services as well as new services and complement existing efforts. Its assessments of high-value health care would be accessible to payers, providers, patients and the public.

Like the Federal Reserve System, it could also include regional health value boards to tap into local medical leadership. Such boards may be better able to gain the trust and change the behavior of local providers than a national board. This Federal health board system could be built on existing State and Federal efforts.

Third, Medicare should become a leader in promoting value. Despite funding less than 20 percent of the health system, Medicare often sets the standards for the private sector. It could lead the shift to a value-based system as well. Congress could delegate authority to Medicare to adopt payment policies consistent with value-oriented standards. Such changes could be allowed within boundaries.

For example, the authority could be limited to changes that would reduce spending within the budget window according to Congressional Budget Office or MedPAC or some authority. Congress could always override these changes, but the default would be flipped. Medicare would automatically adopt value-based policies rather than relying on Congress to do so.

In addition, Medicare could use its capital financing to facilitate high-value care. For example, it could support computer-assisted reminder systems that have proven effective at improving use. It could also make the adoption of such practices part of its accreditation for hospitals and providers.

This infrastructure—and in addition, in my testimony I talk about mandatory health information technology, which could be a part of this, as well as the importance of prioritizing prevention. There are considerable policies out there to figure out how we shift the emphasis from acute care to prevention, and those are detailed in my testimony.

But this infrastructure for standards, information exchange, and tools for its use does not depend exclusively on a private or public insurance system. It could be put into place through incremental reform. But high-value health care cannot be initially or consistently applied when one in three Americans falls out of the system over the course of 2 years; and using public financing to leverage private, value-based care and coverage is necessary to meet the system's potential.

So, in closing, the imperative for improving the value in the health care system is strong, and the opportunity for doing so may be nearer. The next Congress and President face inescapable tax and budget decisions, and a number of expiring policies will be waiting on the doorstep. Tax and budget reform represent an opportunity for health reform, and I am encouraged by your focus on value today.

Thank you for your attention.

[The prepared statement of Jeanne Lambrew follows:]

PREPARED STATEMENT OF JEANNE M. LAMBREW, PH.D., ASSOCIATE PROFESSOR, LYNDON B. JOHNSON SCHOOL OF PUBLIC AFFAIRS, UNIVERSITY OF TEXAS AT AUSTIN

Chairman Spratt, Ranking Member Ryan, and distinguished Members of the Committee, I thank you for the opportunity to testify on the topic of value in health care. Arguably, few other topics are more important to your work. As the Congressional Budget Office Director has testified, the long-run budget problems are largely driven by health cost growth. Medicare, Medicaid, and other health program spending comprise about one-fourth of the Federal budget. Their rapid projected growth accounts for the entire long-run Federal fiscal deficit. It is an economic as well as a budget issue. Health spending accounts for 16 percent of our economy—more than housing or food. Its rapid growth poses challenges to businesses and individuals whose income is increasingly devoted to paying for health care. And, despite the enormous investment in health care, the quality of that care and its outcomes fall short by most standards. As the Federal Reserve Board Chair Ben Bernacke recently said, "Improving the performance of our health-care system is without a doubt one of the most important challenges that our nation faces."

In this testimony, I would like to suggest how value in the health care system can be improved and why the opportunity to do so is on the horizon. "Value" generally describes the perceived quality of care or benefit per dollar spent. Improving value is not necessarily synonymous with improving efficiency. Some aspects of care provision, such as its patient centeredness, are worthwhile to patients but not strictly efficient. Nonetheless, the United States spends an enormous amount on duplicative, low-utility, and even harmful health care, so that a high-value health system would be more efficient overall—and offer significant non-economic advantages as well.

ELEMENTS OF A VALUE-ORIENTED SYSTEM

There is no "silver bullet" for improving value in health care, precisely because of the nature of health care. The exacting rules that govern fields like engineering and physics do not apply to human health. Illnesses and therapies evolve rapidly, with new diseases and cures introduced each year. Basic economic rules also fit some aspects of health care poorly. Technological advances that typically lower labor costs have instead raised them by increasing the reliance on highly-paid health care specialists. Mass production that has revolutionized other sectors has no real foothold in health; health care jobs now outnumber manufacturing jobs.[1] Moreover, people still trust their doctors to define their demand (i.e., diagnose it) as well as fulfill it. People believe high-cost care equals high-quality care, despite evidence to the contrary. And, they undervalue disease prevention and overvalue disease "heroics" or intense medical interventions to reverse disease—reflecting the values and beliefs that also shape our health system.

The nature of health care make it is impossible to draft a single, perfect health care system: it would not work for all providers and people, and even if it did, it would be obsolete quickly. It also means that classical market solutions do not neatly apply to health care. Demand is complicated, providers sit on both the supply and demand sides of the equation, and suppliers—primarily insurers—have little incentive to promote value when payers and enrollees come and go. What is needed instead, in my opinion, is a strong infrastructure though which changing information, best practices, and preferences can be channeled. This infrastructure consists of standards for high-quality, cost-effective care, networks for transferring these standards throughout the system, and policies for their adoption, described below.

Standards for High-Value Health Care: In certain respects, the United States leads the world in health care. The National Institutes of Health, its universities and its private-sector labs have produced medical breakthroughs that have benefited millions and are used worldwide. Some insurers and payers of care have used this information to successfully shape the delivery of care. For example, most health plans use the Healthcare Effectiveness Data and Information Set (HEDIS) that measures plan and provider performance on key quality indicators, with proven success. And, some providers have developed feedback systems to inform both the basic research as well its adaptation for daily practice. For example, Kaiser Permanente's monitoring of its own enrollees detected the increased risk of heart attacks associated with Vioxx and dropped its coverage of it—contributing to its withdrawal from the market. Despite evidence of the benefits and tradeoffs for many if not most treatment options, no authoritative synthesis of such information exists. Instead, different and sometimes conflicting standards are used across the nation, propagated by specialty societies, some government programs, insurers, consumer websites, and regional coalitions.

The consequences of few standards for high-value health care and coverage are troubling. Lack of knowledge of recommended therapies likely contributed to their provision only 55 percent of the time.[2] Another study found that only 41 percent of primary care doctors were familiar with national guidelines for blood pressure treatment, although awareness increased the probability of recommended action.[3] Competing standards also affect performance. For example, a study by the Institute of Medicine found the six major Federal health programs had different quality standards, creating unnecessary confusion and burdens for providers.[4] A typical doctor has public and privately insured patients, making the adherence to the different coverage and quality reporting onerous. And, as can be seen in the studies of practice patterns, the variability is greater for services with a weaker evidence base. For example, the landmark Dartmouth study that found no better quality or outcomes in high-cost areas attributed the excess costs to greater use of testing and evaluative services as well as use of the hospital as a site of care; use of major surgical procedures and minor non-discretionary services were not significantly different.[5] In the absence of evidence on benefits and costs, people and often providers assume that more is better even when it may be wasteful or harmful.

Creating a standard-setting process to guide health care decision making could improve value in the health system. This process could identify services and delivery system practices for which there is: (a) strong evidence for or against their use; (b) strong evidence on the tradeoffs of substitutes; or (c) weak evidence. It could also identify research gaps that should be prioritized to promote a high-performing health system. In particular, studies on the comparative clinical and cost effectiveness of different treatment options could be encouraged. These standards would neither constitute "cook-book medicine" nor the elements for a defined benefits plan. For example, the process would not weigh in on resource allocation and who pays for care. Instead, these standards would advance a common understanding of the state-of-the-art health care practices—the basic building block for improving performance.

Information Exchange Networks: Dissemination is as critical as the development of standards. Standards can only affect performance if they reach the remote parts of our health system, and vice versa: information and expertise from all parts of the health system are needed to set the standards. Historically, knowledge among providers and managers has been shared through annual conferences, continuing medical education programs, journals, and specialty societies. Disease registries, where information is collected on certain types of patients and treatment protocols, have proven to assist in both education and adoption. The rapid evolution of information technology has also facilitated dissemination and adaptation at all levels of the health system. "Learning networks" and Regional Health Insurance Exchanges have been created to harmonize data collection and reporting at the local level. Provider and consumer decision support tools have proliferated. And the interest in implementing a nationwide electronic medical record is strong.

Yet, rather than simplifying the system, the explosion of communication tools has sometimes increased chaos. Internet-based journals, physician and health plan resources, and consumer resources (e.g., WebMD) abound. A patchwork of registries and data bases has placed time-consuming and sometimes expensive demands on providers and organizations to participate. Entrepreneurs have entered the space, offering electronic health records, support systems, and feedback tools. Meanwhile, there is no evidence that these advances have shortened the years for a proven treatment to move from the lab bench to the bedside. And, a recent study found that only 4 percent of physicians used a complete electronic medical record, with an additional 13 percent using a basic system.[6]

One key step to increasing value in health care is creating a national, health information technology infrastructure to facilitate development and dissemination of best practices. Beyond its potential administrative savings, information technology could build in prompts, reminders, and error warnings at the point of service. The Veterans' Administration health system has used technology in this way with positive results. In addition, a national, privacy-protected electronic health record would provide data for studies on the comparative effects of clinical and delivery system interventions on a wide-scale basis. This could make the health system more efficient over time by limiting the adoption of new therapies that offer less benefit than existing ones.[7] Technology is an essential but not the sole source for the exchange of information. The heavy reliance on judgment and experience in health care delivery supports the idea of building regional peer networks. Like specialty societies, they would provide the latest research and data feedback, but would do so with an understanding of the local context, culture, and health system resources.

Tools to Promote Adoption of High-Value Care: Arguably the greatest challenge to promoting value is ensuring that the participants in the system adhere to proven standards. Knowledge of these standards alone can help. But, evidence suggests it is not enough. Regular blood testing is a well-known standard of care for diabetics, yet only 24 percent of participants in a national study had three or more glycosylated hemoglobin tests over a two-year period.[8] Conversely, there is little evidence supporting the use of CT scans for management of heart disease yet a recent article documented the rapid increase in their use and thus costs.[9]

Part of this pattern can be explained by reimbursement rates. Value is rarely taken into account when determining whether and what a provider gets paid.[10] Payment rates usually only account for a service's cost, not its benefits—promoting high-cost health care irrespective of its merit. This may explain why there is higher adherence to standards of care for procedures (which tend to have high reimbursement) versus counseling (which tends to go unreimbursed).[11] Similarly, the amount that patients pay in cost sharing is typically pegged to a service's cost rather than its value. Simply stated, financial incentives for providers and patients are misaligned.

Beyond financing, the lack of organization of the delivery system diffuses the accountability for producing value. Studies have found that having an organizational culture that promotes quality results in high performance ratings for providers.[12] Yet, most doctors still practice alone or in small groups and lack the critical mass to implement and connect to larger systems to improve the value of the care for their patients. Ideas to remedy this range from linking all providers to a hospital to forging "interdependent practice organizations" that assume responsibility for members' performance.[13] Beyond their ability to invest in system supports, organizations could also have a social network effect on provider behavior, which has recently been found to be powerful in reducing obesity and tobacco use.[14]

Lastly, an often-overlooked tool in improving value is making it the path of least resistance. A growing literature suggests that making the desired behavior the default improves the odds of achieving it.[15] For example, the use of beta blockers after a heart attack is the standard of care. Research has found greater use of this drug among patients to whom it was prescribed in the hospital discharge orders—not leaving it to the patient to fill the prescription independently later. Moreover, some hospitals automatically prescribe beta blockers on the discharge order, allowing the doctor to take it off the order, but asking for an explanation why. This system reduces the required steps needed to achieve the desired result. Across the board, payment and delivery systems could be designed so that high-value care is the easiest choice for individuals and providers.[16]

POLICIES TO CREATE THE INFRASTRUCTURE FOR A VALUE-ORIENTED SYSTEM

This infrastructure—standards for value, information exchange networks, and tools for its use—could undergird different mixes of public and private insurance. It does not depend on either an exclusively public or private insurance system to work. As such, it could be incorporated into a number of different health reform plans. However, a key to achieving a high-value health system is seamless coverage for all Americans: high-value care cannot be initially or consistently applied when one in three individuals falls out of the system for at least a month over a two-year period.[17] Similarly, inadequate coverage—a problem for 25 million insured Americans according to a recent study—results in cost-related barriers to care and coordination and communications problems which interfere with value-oriented care.[18] As Henry Aaron has put it, ensuring adequate coverage for all Americans is, "a precondition for effective measures to limit overall health care spending."[19]

That said, some of the infrastructure for a value-oriented health system could be put into place in the context of incremental reform. These components are described below.

Investing in Comparative Effectiveness Research: A pre-requisite to assigning value in health care is knowing various services' relative impact. "Comparative effectiveness research" is the rigorous assessment of the relative safety, effectiveness, and cost of treatments or approaches for addressing the same condition. This type of research has been funded by the Agency for Healthcare Research and Quality's (AHRQ's) appropriations, but at a fraction of the amount authorized in the Medicare drug law enacted in 2003. Proposals to significantly increase comparative effectiveness research funding and ensure its independence have support from a wide range of businesses, consumer groups, and experts, including the health advisor to George H.W. Bush.[20] Bipartisan legislation has been introduced by Representatives Allen and Emerson and a version of it was included in the Children's Health and Medicare Protections Act of 2007 that passed the House but was vetoed by President

Bush. The Congressional Budget Office estimated that this provision, which created a trust fund seeded by public and private funding, would save the system $6 billion over 10 years and reduce Federal spending by the tenth year.[21] The 111th Congress should enact this legislation since this information is essential to setting standards for value.

Creating a Federal Reserve-Like Board to Set Standards: Another policy to consider is the creation of an independent board to promote high-value health care.[22] Composed of experts with long terms, this board would be modeled on the Federal Reserve Board which has succeeded in making crucial decisions with greater credibility than most Federal agencies. This board would be an authoritative source of information on the value and tradeoffs of health care services and delivery mechanisms. Because of the breadth of health care, the board would focus on high-cost and new services. To ensure it complements rather than replaces existing efforts, it could give its imprimatur to publicly and privately-developed standards (e.g., U.S. Preventive Services Task Force guidelines; the AHRQ's Evidence-Based Practice Centers; the National Quality Forum; specialty societies' protocols). Its assessments of high-value health care would be accessible to payers, providers, patients, and the public.

The board would also assess the optimal mode for delivering high-value care. This function may be best carried out regionally. The Federal Reserve has twelve district banks whose governance includes key stakeholders as well as experts. They are responsive to their regional resources and climate—features that could be valuable in promoting value given the geographic variation in health care. Regional "health value" boards could tap into medical leadership to tailor their work to region-specific problems. They could gather data, analyze it for patterns, and feed the results back to providers and facilities with comparisons to local, regional and national process and outcome measures. They may be better able to gain the trust and change the behavior of local providers than a national board. Several states have already developed regional consortia to promote quality and efficiency.[23] These boards could also be built from the current Quality Improvement Organizations in Medicare. Medicare could support regional boards by providing data as well as incentives (or requirements) that providers participate in them.

Accelerating the Use of Health Information Technology: This Congress may succeed in enacting legislation that creates standards, privacy protections, and funding for the implementation of electronic health records (EHRs). The bipartisan legislation is necessary but probably not sufficient to yield rapid adoption of EHRs in a short period of time. Physicians may still be resistant given their inability to capture the return on the investment; private plans may worry about losing a competitive edge; and the benefits that result may make it more of a public good that private commodity.[24] Congress should consider making the President's aspiration that most Americans have an EHR by 2014 a deadline. It could enforce this requirement in a number of ways, including lower or no Medicare payment to providers who do not comply. Loans and grants would likely be needed to assist in meeting this deadline. The ongoing activity to set standards for interoperability and privacy and create data exchanges to support EHRs would need to be stepped up. Other nations have already made the switch from paper-based to electronic systems; it is feasible as well as essential to optimizing health system performance.

Allowing Medicare to Align Policies with Value: Even though it funds less than 20 percent of the health system, Medicare's policies have often set the standard for the private sector. The shift to a new standard based on value could be led by Medicare as well. Congress could delegate authority to Medicare to adopt payment policies that the Medicare Payment Advisory Commission recommends based on the value-oriented standards set by the new board. These changes could include adopting successful "pay for performance" models, creating bundled payments across providers and/or services, and adjusting patient cost sharing to promote high-value care and discourage low-value care. Such changes could be allowed within boundaries; for example, the authority could be limited to modifications that reduce spending within the budget window according to the Congressional Budget Office. The Medicare Trustees might also take a bigger role in program operation, having to approve the policies recommended by the program administrator. Congress could always override the changes, but the default would be flipped: instead of having to wait for Congress to align payments with value, Medicare would do so unless Congress blocked it.

In addition, Medicare payment systems build in some funding for capital improvements; this funding could be directed toward system design to facilitate high-value care. For example, Medicare could incentivize hospitals to develop or adopt computer-assisted reminder or default order systems that have proven effective at improving adherence and outcomes. It could also add the use of effective, simplifying systems as a condition of accreditation; arguably, they are as important to safety and the system as a facilities' cleanliness or doctor attendance at medical staff meetings.

Prioritizing Prevention: Lastly, the gravity of the problem of preventable disease, coupled with the inadequacy of the existing system, suggests that a new model is needed to prioritize wellness. To be effective, it should strive to make preventive services valued by individuals and providers, available, and affordable. It should elevate wellness within the health system and complement it with new delivery systems. Payment for prevention should be designed to leverage behavioral change and widespread use. Finally, it should be universal, providing recommended prevention services irrespective of individuals' insurance status.

A Wellness Trust is one approach for structuring an effective prevention system.[25] Under this model, preventive services would be carved out of the health insurance system and financed through a new independent agency. The Wellness Trust would set national priorities for prevention, employ unconventional systems for delivering services, use payment policy to drive results, and integrate prevention with the health care system through information technology. Congress could lay the groundwork for this approach by creating the Trust, assessing prevention spending, reviewing priorities, and developing a prevention workforce.

OPPORTUNITY

The imperative for improving value in the health system is strong, and the opportunity to do so may be near. The next Congress and president face inescapable tax and budget—as well as health policy—decisions. A number of expiring policies will be waiting on the doorstep. These include: the 2001 and 2003 tax cuts, the escalating taxes due to the Alternative Minimum Tax problem, and a budget that will likely be unresolved in 2008. Tax and budget reform represents an opportunity for health reform. Responsible tax policy to replace the expiring Bush tax cuts could build in revenue to fund up-front health system changes. Modifying while maintaining the tax break for employer health benefits could redirect high-income tax breaks to low-income tax credits.[26] And, the cost savings inherent in health reform are essential to long-run budget stability.

No doubt, enacting health—and budget and tax—reform is hard. Yet, the only thing harder may be turning a blind eye while our nation's health and economic prospects fade. Incremental reform can lay the groundwork for a high-quality, efficient, equitable health system; the policies described here take steps toward it. But small changes may take as much political capital as big ones. A strong infrastructure must be combined with coverage in a seamless system supported by sustainable financing to achieve the potential of a high-value health system.

ENDNOTES

[1] For a discussion of labor costs and the health sector, see, for example, J. Hartwig. (March 2006). What Drives Health Care Expenditures? Baumol's Model of Unbalanced Growth Revisited. KOF Swiss Economic Institute, ETH Zurich, Working paper number 06-133. *http://www.kof.ethz.ch/publications/science/pdf/wp—133.pdf*

[2] E. McGlynn et al. (2003). "The Quality of Care Delivered to Adults in the United States," New England Journal of Medicine,348 (26): 2634-45.

[3] D.J. Hyman and V.N. Pavlik. (2000). "Self-Reported Hypertension Treatment Practices Among Primary Care Doctors," Archives of Internal Medicine,160: 2281-86.

[4] J. Corrigan, J. Eden, B.M. Smith. (2003). Leadership by Example: Coordinating Government's Role in Improving Health Care Quality. Washington, DC: National Academies Press.

[5] E.S. Fisher et al. (2003). "The Implications of Regional Variation in Medicare Part I: The Content, Quality, and Accessibility of Care," Archives of Internal Medicine,138: 273-87.

[6] C.M. DesRoches et al. (July 3, 2008). "Electronic Health Records in Ambulatory Care: A National Survey of Physicians," New England Journal of Medicine, 350:50-60.

[7] For a discussion of the potential impact of health information technology on cost, see Congressional Budget Office. (May 2008). Evidence on the Costs and Benefits of Health Information Technology. Washington, DC: CBO.

[8] E. McGlynn et al. (2003). "The Quality of Care Delivered to Adults in the United States," New England Journal of Medicine,348 (26): 2634-45.

[9] A. Berenson and R. Abelson. (June 29, 2008). "The Evidence Gap: Weighing the Costs of a CT Scan's Look Inside the Heart," The New York Times,A1.

[10] Value is not a component of public program payment systems, and a recent survey found few employers use it. See: M.B. Rosenthal et al. (2007). "Employers' Use of Value-Based Purchasing Strategies," JAMA, 298(19): 2281-88.

[11] E. McGlynn et al. (2003). "The Quality of Care Delivered to Adults in the United States," New England Journal of Medicine,348 (26): 2634-45.

[12] See, for example, S.M. Shortell et al. (2005). "An Empirical Assessment of High-Performing Medical Groups: Results from a National Study," Medical Care Research and Review, 62(4): 407-34.

[13] See, for example, E.S. Fisher et al. (2007). "Creating Accountable Health Care Organizations: The Extended Hospital Medical Staff," Health Affairs, 26(1): w44-w57; S.M. Shortell, L.P. Casalino. (2008). "Health Care Reform Requires Accountable Organizations," JAMA, 300(1): 95-97.

[14] A recent article discussed several of the emerging studies: R. Stein. (May 26, 2008). "Social Networks' Sway May be Underestimated," Washington Post, A06.

[15] For a discussion of behavioral economics and its possible application to health care, see P. Orszag. (2008). "Health Care and Behavioral Economics: A Presentation to the National Academy of Social Insurance," Washington, DC: Congressional Budget Office.

[16] For a commentary on how this might be done, see B. James. (2001). "Making It Easy to Do It Right," New England Journal of Medicine, 345: 991-93.

[17] J.A. Rhoades and S.B. Cohen. (August 2007). "The Long-Term Uninsured in America, 2002-2005," Rockville, MD: U.S. DHHS, AHRQ, Statistical Brief #183.

[18] C. Schoen et al. (2008). "How Many Are Underinsured? Trends Among U.S. Adults, 2003 and 2007," Health Affairs, WebExclusive, 27(4): w298-309.

[19] H. Aaron. (2007). "Budget Crisis, Entitlement Crisis, Health Care Financing Problem—Which Is It?" Health Affairs, 26 (6): 1622-33.

[20] G.R. Wilensky. (2006). "Developing a Center for Comparative Effectiveness Information," Health Affairs, 25(6): w572-85.

[21] See P. Orszag. (September 7, 2007). "Letter to Chairman Pete Stark," Washington, DC: Congressional Budget Office, available at: *http://www.cbo.gov/ftpdocs/85xx/doc8598/09-05-ComparativeEffectiveness.pdf*

[22] This idea is the subject of a book: T. Daschle, with S.S. Greenberger and J.M. Lambrew. (2008). Critical: What We Can Do About the Health Care Crisis. New York: St. Martin's Press.

[23] See, for example, Minnesota's SmartBuy Alliance. A coalition of purchasers accounting for 60-70 percent of the State's population, its members use uniform performance standards, cost and quality reporting requirements, and technology. S. Silow-Carroll and T. Alteras. (2007). Value-Driven Health Care Purchasing: Case Study of Minnesota's Smart Buy Alliance. New York: The Commonwealth Fund.

[24] Congressional Budget Office. (May 2008). Evidence on the Costs and Benefits of Health Information Technology. Washington, DC: CBO.

[25] For details, see: J.M. Lambrew and J.D. Podesta. (2006). Promoting Prevention and Preempting Costs: A New Wellness Trust for the United States. Washington, DC: Center for American Progress; and J.M. Lambrew. (2007). A Wellness Trust to Prioritize Disease Prevention. Washington, DC: The Brookings Institution, The Hamilton Project.

[26] For a discussion of financing options, see M. Seshamani, J.M. Lambrew, and J.R. Antos. (2008). Financing the U.S. Health System: Issues and Options for Change. Washington, DC: Bipartisan Policy Center.

Chairman SPRATT. Dr. Gratzer.

STATEMENT OF DAVID GRATZER, M.D., SENIOR FELLOW, MANHATTAN INSTITUTE FOR POLICY RESEARCH

Dr. GRATZER. Thank you, Mr. Chairman, ranking member, members of the committee.

I have provided you with written testimony which provides some thought on these topics. I would emphasize that though I am a Senior Fellow at the Manhattan Institute, the views I express in that written testimony, as well as today, are my views and my views alone, and don't necessarily reflect those of the Manhattan Institute.

Mr. Chairman, health care can be enormously personal. I think it is perhaps one of the reasons we are discussing it here today. Besides, obviously, the budgetary implications, there are other aspects of public policy that are enormously important, but perhaps none quite as personal as health care. Let me open then by talking personally about some of my experiences with American health care and then maybe drawing some larger lessons.

It was the best of American medicine, the worst of American health care. My wife hurt her back. I would emphasize my wife tells this story slightly differently than I do. For the sake of our marriage, I have that disclosure.

I was invited to a conference out in the Rockies. They very generously agreed to pay for my ski ticket and the airfare. All I had to do was buy a pass for my wife. She ended up on a ski slope and hurt her back.

I would emphasize she tells this story differently than I do.

My version of events involves a Bunny Hill, a ski school—perhaps the Snoopy Dog Ski Camp or something august like that—with a lot of 5-year-olds, who, by the way, were absolutely marvelous skiers. And my wife fell a lot.

She tells this story involving a large mountain, gale-like winds of about 70 miles per hour, and a small furry mammal that had to be avoided, perhaps a squirrel or something of this sort. But the long and the short of it is, my wife ruptured a disc in her back.

My wife is an emergency doctor, and she went from living an extraordinarily active life to lying on her back hours a day because of the pain. Of course, there was the numbness in her foot which made work very difficult.

She needed a procedure. We are two doctors. At the time, for a variety of reasons, we were living in West New York and we weren't insured, and we were trying to find the best care we could. Well, we are tech-savvy people. We went to Yahoo. We are not super-tech-savvy people because we would have Googled, I suspect, but we Yahooed, and the top 10 sites were pornographic.

Finally, we found a neurosurgeon we were comfortable with. We were interested in outcomes. We couldn't find any on the Internet. He couldn't provide us with any. We had a choice of two hospitals for this procedure. We decided, not being able to get any quality data, to choose the one with "saint" in the title, because, as you know, Mr. Chairman, nothing bad can happen to you at a hospital with "saint" in the title.

These are some of the frustrations we experienced.

We also experienced frustrations around the bill. At the end of the day we were sent a bill that was a foot-and-a-half long, and it was my medical opinion that they didn't know what they were talking about. I called up the top administrator of the hospital, and I said, I have never not paid a bill in my life, but this seems outrageous for a day procedure. She responded by telling me that this is simply the starting point of our negotiations.

I don't know anywhere else in American society where you get a bill from somebody and they fully acknowledge that they themselves don't take the bill seriously.

I also want to emphasize, though, that this was the best of American medicine. Fifty years ago somebody like my wife would have hurt her back and would have lived out the rest of her life with chronic pain and some significant morbidity. Twenty years ago I suppose she would have had a spinal fusion, which is a very complicated procedure.

Today, or a few years ago, she got a procedure that lasted under half an hour, an incision that was less than an inch, and she is up and about and living her life as she wants to. We had our second child a year ago and life is good. That is the best of American medicine. We can never forget that when we have these discussions. These are always feel-bad discussions.

I don't feel badly about American medicine and I don't feel badly about the future because we have done so much in the last 60 years—tamed polio, made depression treatable, allowed people like my wife to return to the workforce—and I look very much forward to what we will do over the next 60 years. Part of the reason we were able to do these things is that we have certain values in American health care that we should preserve even when we talk about what is wrong with it.

First and foremost is that we value the doctor-patient relationship. Secondly is that we recognize that not all decisions should be driven by dollars and cents, that health care also has some intuitive value. And thirdly, perhaps a point slightly underappreciated, is the best way of spending money often is keeping people out of the health care system, by which I mean keeping them healthy in the first place.

There are undoubtedly enormous problems with American health care. Costs keep rising year after year. My colleague and cowitness has given a very nice summary of some of the macro implications.

I like to think of things in terms of its implications in the American family. As you know, every year for the last 7 years the median family income has dropped by about 1,000 bucks a year because of rising health costs, even though wages are up.

These are enormous problems. What should we do to get better value in American health care? Well, I put forward a number of ideas. But, again, I think back to my wife and that black box of American health care that we dealt with, and I think forward to some basic ideas.

First of all, we need to move decisions closer to families. Too much of American health care, for historic reasons, is paid by someone else, usually employers, and, of course, as you are well aware also, the Federal and State governments. I like experiments like health savings accounts. I like Medicaid experiments like those going on in South Carolina and Florida, again bringing decisions closer to the individual.

Transparency is, I think, something we can all agree has enormous value. I would point out, though, that even though the Federal Government sits on such a wealth of information, relatively little of it is revealed.

I would also suggest that if we are talking about the government pushing the private sector in more of the right direction, we could talk about better disclosure by hospitals, clinics and doctors in terms of fee schedules and the like.

We need better information on quality, and I think that is a thorny issue. Often it is difficult for us to judge how to do that. Certainly, with surgeries, one can look at complications, and that is relatively straightforward. But I am a psychiatrist, and sometimes I wonder how one judges who is a good psychiatrist and who isn't.

I think some of this information is going to come from the public sector. I think about the New York State report cards on cardiac surgery. Some of it will come from the private sector, such as the Leapfrog Group and their work.

Finally, I believe in five-sixths of the general economy, we have discovered that the best way of improving quality and value is through competition and choice, and too often in health care, governments have been eager to regulate first and ask questions later. It deprives individuals of choice, innovation suffers, and I think, ultimately costs rise.

I would suggest to you those are some basic commonsense ideas we can employ with health care to move us forward so that people like my wife and I can have better information on quality before we make a decision, people like my wife and I and you and your spouse and your constituents.

Thank you very much.

Ms. SCHWARTZ [presiding]. Okay, and thank you for your testimony.

[The prepared statement of David Gratzer follows:]

PREPARED STATEMENT OF DAVID GRATZER, M.D., MANHATTAN INSTITUTE

I am honored to testify today in these hearings on "Getting Better Value in Health Care" before the Committee on the Budget. My name is David Gratzer. I am a physician and a senior fellow at the Manhattan Institute in New York. The views I present are my own and do not necessarily represent those of the Manhattan Institute.

Before speaking directly to the topic at hand, I wish to put forward an important anecdote. The daughter of a friend of my family will start elementary school in the fall. Of course, there doesn't seem much remarkable about the above statement—millions of children across the United States are starting grade 1 in a couple of months. But my friend's daughter is a cancer survivor. Just a couple of years ago, she was diagnosed with leukemia. After a series of treatments, however, she's fine. Actually, she's more than fine. She's bright, energetic, full of life. And why shouldn't she be?

But not that long ago, of course, a diagnosis of childhood leukemia was a death sentence. Today, the vast majority of children under the age of 12 with this illness are cured. That's not to suggest that life isn't without complications—recent studies peg their SAT scores at lower than average for their age cohort—but these challenges seem minor compared to battling cancer.

We're talking today about "getting better value in health care." At a time when health costs are spiraling up, it would be difficult to think of a more timely or relevant topic. But as we consider what's wrong with American health care and what's to do, it's important to remember what's right. People like my friend's daughter get excellent health care.

Before discussing better value, we should note our values in making it possible for people like my friend's daughter to thrive: (1) American health care is built on the doctor-patient relationship; (2) health care isn't just about dollars and cents, but about improving lives; (3) the best way of saving money is to keep people out of the health care system by keeping them healthy in the first place.

We live in challenging times. My co-witness Peter Orszag provided macro-numbers pointing out the high cost of health care. Let me bring things back to the household level: Median family income has dropped by a thousand dollars a year every year since the beginning of the decade because of rising health costs.

Why? The central problem is the way Americans pay for their care. Rather than paying directly, most people get their health insurance from their employer (or the parent's or spouse's employer). Someone else foots the bill. This odd financing arrangement developed because of World War II wage controls. Employers began to provide health benefits as a disguised form of income, and their incentive to do so only increased when the IRS ruled that, unlike income, these employer-provided benefits would not be taxed.

The resulting accidental system is wasteful and bureaucratic. With Americans paying directly just 13 cents for every health dollar they spend, there is much incentive to spend first, and ask questions later. Health managers, meanwhile, create bureaucratic hurdles in an attempt to constrain patient choice (and thus costs). During the 1990s-heyday of managed care, for instance, HMOs attempted to dictate whether and when their patients were tested. HMOs have fallen away—the economic problem they attempted to address continues.

There is hope: the Miami Herald ran a story on a Fort Lauderdale woman who shopped around for physiotherapy—and saved herself a thousand dollars a session. Obviously, not every health service can be "shopped for." That said, there are some basic steps that we should take with health care to make it easier for patients and providers to seek out excellence and value:

MOVING DECISIONS CLOSER TO FAMILIES

Innovative health insurance products like health savings accounts encourage Americans to think more about the financial consequences (and the value) of the health services they receive. Medicaid experiments in South Carolina and Florida also attempt to reward better decisions.

TRANSPARENCY

For practically everything other than health care, Americans are able to access good pricing information before making a decision. That's not true with health care. HHS has started to reveal more information—an important if small step. The federal government should make its pricing information available and encourage hospitals, clinics, and doctors to do the same.

BETTER INFORMATION ON QUALITY

While some aspects of health care remain difficult to measure, surgical outcomes, complication rates, and a raft of other information is available—except to patients. Ultimately, better quality information should be developed, which probably will come from both public sector sources (e.g., the New York State report cards on cardiac surgery) and private sources (e.g., the Leapfrog Group).

MORE COMPETITION AND CHOICE

For 60 years, the federal and state governments have heavily regulated health care. The end result is that patients are deprived of choice, innovation suffers and costs ultimately rise. New regulations ought to be carefully considered in terms of their impact on choice; existing regulations should be reviewed.

Some have suggested that a centralized board should oversee health-care decisions. While the idea is tempting—who wouldn't want a defining authority to push America to better value in health care?—the international results are at best mixed. The euphemistically named NICE in Britain, as an example, is slow to approve drugs for funding (often taking up to 2 years) and tremendously biased against new or cutting-edge cancer treatments, which partially explains the poor outcomes found in that country.

American medicine has never been better. American health care, though, is at a cross-roads. Some see utility in pushing down the path to greater government involvement. In five-sixth of the economy, however, we value individual choice, competition, and responsibility. The prescription for American health care is thus clear.

Ms. SCHWARTZ. I guess I have the discretion of the Chair, which is kind of neat, so I think I was first in line to ask questions anyway, so if my colleagues will indulge.

I did want to thank you again very much for your testimony. I think one of the themes that came out in all of your testimony was the issue of quality. That has come up. I particularly wanted, though, to focus my question on something else that two of you mentioned, which is the issue of health IT.

We had a very good win I think for Medicare and for the country last evening when we passed the Medicare bill, which included e-Prescribing, an initiative of mine that I know all of you know about, that is a great first step in using health information technology, moving doctors and hospitals to use that technology to reduce errors, to save lives and to save money.

So what I would like you to do is elaborate, if you will. And I know there was some work—Peter Orszag, you particularly have done some study of this.

But I wanted to also ask, Jeanne Lambrew, if you will comment on the potential for improving quality, improving health outcomes for Americans, if we were to scale up in a very aggressive way the use of information technology, particularly electronic medical records; and specifically how we might do that other than just your suggestion of mandating it, which I guess is one possibility.

But my question very clearly is, what do you believe we should do right away on information technology and electronic medical records in particular? And how could that impact both savings in the health care system, the public and providers, and improve outcomes?

Dr. Orszag, if you would start, that would be great.

Mr. ORSZAG. Sure, Chairwoman, I will elaborate a little bit.

Let me say first that health IT has substantial potential to help reduce costs and improve quality in health care if—if—it is part of a system in which the information is used to evaluate what works and what doesn't, and if it is part of a system in which there are financial incentives for the stuff that works.

But just by itself, plopping a health IT system into a fragmented system with distorted financial incentives and no way of using the information in general doesn't generate the kinds of results that many people would hope for.

Ms. SCHWARTZ. So does that involve, Federal standards have to come first, or be a part of it, as to how they will be used?

Mr. ORSZAG. There are questions about interoperability and what have you, and I will leave that aside for a second.

What I meant was the evidence on health IT actually generating improvements in efficiency or some combination of higher quality and lower costs are more impressive for more integrated systems where the information that's coming out of a system is used to evaluate the procedures and then to push back down to the practitioners some guidance on what works and what doesn't.

In an isolated hospital setting or an isolated physician setting, we have much less opportunity to do that, unless the information is then garnered or used for some broader comparative effectiveness kind of effort.

Ms. SCHWARTZ. Certainly systems that use it say that, in and of itself, the use of electronic medical records, particularly if they are interoperable, actually do help alleviate the fragmentation, basically help to coordinate care, because your doctor can see work that has been done last week by another doctor, your emergency room can see your test results from your doctors the week before.

So it actually forces, if you want to call it that, a better integrated system. I don't know if you want to comment on that, or Professor Lambrew.

Go ahead.

Mr. ORSZAG. I would just say—I guess she is deferring to me for a second—on the fragmentation, the problem is really the financial incentives and the way in which care can be delivered in multiple settings. Yes, you can get some benefit from seeing the tests that were done somewhere else, but that is not the most salient or problematic aspect of fragmentation.

The biggest problem associated with fragmentation is that you have financial incentives for multiple care being done in multiple places without the kind of unification that doesn't come just from seeing the other tests that were done.

Ms. SCHWARTZ. You are saying, even if they see the MRI from yesterday, they are still going to repeat it because there is no financial disincentive.

I am not sure that is true, by the way, but that is what you are saying, isn't it?

Mr. ORSZAG. You assumed, also, full interoperability. In many cases that is not the case. So unless you have full interoperability and then, again, some system for—it is not just whether they repeat the MRI, but whether the MRI is used.

When the MRI is done or not done could be informed by, how many times for that kind of patient does the MRI change the diagnosis. And unless you have some structure in place for evaluating that kind of information, just stringing together lots of different outpatient settings where there are MRIs done and letting them see each other's MRIs is not going to change that basic dynamic.

Ms. SCHWARTZ. But, again, the issue is also the software that suggests you ought to order the MRI or you don't need to. You haven't mentioned that, but that is also part of this, that there is also the opportunity.

And maybe this is the chance, Dr. Lambrew, to jump in to actually be able to say it matters to do an MRI or it matters to talk to somebody at this point about other testing or other kinds of behavior. It is also something that could be part of electronic medical records, based on evidence-based medicine, obviously.

Ms. LAMBREW. I would just say, if we think about the potential benefits of all electronic health records, there are four different levels. There is the basic administrative paperwork savings and reductions, which is important—not necessarily a major driver of our costs, but an important component.

Second, is this information sharing to reduce duplication and to ensure, when possible, coordination? I have to say, as somebody who has tried to gather my medical records because I moved recently, it is not easy. It is not easy to go every third Tuesday to a doctor's office to collect your medical records and pay $25.

So I do think there is more potential to that information sharing than not.

Third is——

Ms. SCHWARTZ. The point is well taken. It is information sharing not only between the providers, but also with the patients and consumers as well.

Ms. LAMBREW. A third level is this idea of using information tools, because in that waterfall of medical information that comes out, physicians and patients, it is hard to figure out what is the right information, how to use it, and do you have it at the bedside at the right moment for both the patient and provider. And using the tools that are available through an information basis or a platform could be significant when we again decide what is high-value care and promoting it.

Lastly—and I feel very strongly about this as a researcher—are the feedback loops. It is trying to figure out how we get the information to feed back in to figure out what is high-value care. You look at two examples of organizations that have used it, the Veterans Administration and Kaiser Permanente. Kaiser discovered Vioxx earlier than anybody else, the problems with it, because it had a system that it could monitor what was going on and pick up and detect things that it wasn't necessarily looking for.

So I think these four levels are the potential for it, and I would argue that we can't get to a system using the word "system" without this basis.

So it is necessary, but not sufficient, to use a cliche.

Ms. SCHWARTZ. Just take another minute to make a comment.

Dr. GRATZER. These comments have been pretty innocuous. I think we would all agree that there is something wrong with a health care system whose basic information infrastructure harkens back to the days of the Pony Express.

Looking internationally, there are countries that have done far more in terms of information technology experimentation. In Canada, Alberta, one of the largest and most affluent provinces, in fact, puts practically all health records now online. You see your family doctor, the tests go on your record; you cross the street and go to the hospital, and it is there and accessible.

In Denmark, they have gone so far as to put the health records online, and it is accessible, in fact, to patients. And patients can even track things like their own cholesterol levels and glucose levels. I think these things are definitely worth thinking about.

I think, again, by the way, some of this will begin in the United States through the private sector. I wonder about Google medicine and Google health. I think it is worth for Congress to weigh these things as well.

I would point out, though, in both the Canadian and Danish experiments, you don't quite get the cost savings that people have suggested you would. I think this might be a step in the right direction. I don't think anyone would argue it is a panacea.

Ms. SCHWARTZ. All right. I would say that what a couple of you are suggesting is that, while it may not be a panacea, it is a tool that we ought to really look seriously at.

There are some conditions set and there are a number of bills moving through Congress thinking about this. But I think we would all really appreciate hearing the conditions that have been suggested as important to this, in and of themselves.

It only matters if we actually do it right, and that is true for just about everything we do. But it is a tool we have not used in any elaborate way. I think less than about 5 percent of American doctors use full electronic medical records. The suggestion is, if done right, it could actually affect both quality outcomes and costs.

We are looking for savings wherever we can get them, and if we can improve quality at the same time, it certainly seems worthwhile.

But having taken my time, I would like to move on and ask Mr. Ryan if he chooses to inquire.

Mr. RYAN. Thank you, Ms. Schwartz. First, let me start off.

Dr. Orszag, you are taking about an hour out of your day, and the rest of the day you are going to be spending on the GSE issue, Fannie and Freddie.

Mr. ORSZAG. I am viewing this hearing as a welcome respite from that.

Mr. RYAN. I am sorry about that. I am going to ask a GSE question, a very brief one, and then I want to get into health care. It is just so topical right now.

I am reading in the Business section of The New York Times today this article that more or less implies that because Treasury is asking for unlimited limits on explicit debt or line of credit or ability to go purchase instruments, that there might not be any score attributed to that.

You are in the middle of trying to score all of this. I am not going to ask you to give specifics because you are probably still figuring this out. But whatever we do on the GSEs, your granting the Treasury more authority, is it not going to score? And if there is no limit to Treasury's ability to go and do this, that is going to score a lot, is it not?

So can you just give me your sense of the wisdom of the implication in this New York Times article? And what should we begin to expect on scores coming from CBO with respect to these ideas we are looking at that we very well could be voting on as early as, I think, Wednesday or something like that.

Mr. ORSZAG. I guess my response would be, that was not news that was fit to print.

Mr. RYAN. The New York Times put that out.

Mr. ORSZAG. Correct.

Mr. RYAN. Okay. Thank you.

Mr. ORSZAG. And that the absence of a limit on the ability of the Treasury to inject funds, either as equity or debt in loans into the GSEs, does not mean in any way that there would be no cost associated, no score associated with the activities. And CBO will be issuing a cost estimate for the legislation in the near term.

Mr. RYAN. All right. I won't ask you any more details, because I am sure you are still figuring that out.

Mr. ORSZAG. Thank you.

Mr. RYAN. I want to, but I won't. Let's go to health care.

There is a bipartisan issue out here that we can get done, and it is IT and it is transparency. So let's explore how we should go about doing this. America is sort of behind the times when it comes to these issues, especially on technology.

First, let me put a pitch in for a bill I have with Dennis Moore on health IT. Right now, the system that works today, you have the marketplace basically putting up silos. You've got McKesson, Epic, Cerner, GE and, I think, Siemens as the main providers of health IT software and hardware, who by their own very designs have these stovepipes where they can't talk to each other. So, by design, they are not interoperable systems.

When you get into this issue, we are concerned about privacy, about the property, who houses these records, individual medical privacy, but also interoperability. So I hope Dennis will take time in his questioning to go into this.

But this is something we are really going to have to look at with respect to how these medical records are housed, where they are housed, who has them, and how do we drive interoperability.

I think, Dr. Orszag, you have given us some good ideas about how to get this going and get it off its feet.

Let me get to the more sticky issue of transparency. In my roadmap plan, I pursue a legislative course, which I will be doing an independent bill on soon, to try to get at real transparency on cost, on price and value and best practices.

And here is the basic question: What is the best way to go about this? Should we have the Federal Government, HHS, CMS, design the metrics on price, design the metrics on quality, design the metrics on best practices; and basically tell physicians how to practice medicine, and we are going to pay you for this or we are going to pay you for that?

The reason I urge caution on this is, from being on the Ways and Means Committee for the last decade, this then becomes politicized. There are just no two ways about it. What you will have are various provider groups, various interest groups come to the Ways and Means Committee and say, pick us as the winner, pick us as favorites; and we nonphysicians will inject ourselves into the practice of medicine in the marketplace. The professionals won't be the decision-makers, it will be the bureaucrats and the politicians.

I think there is probably a better way. And the way we are advocating, and I would like your response to, is, instead of having CMS design and police all of this—which will be behind in the times, it will be behind in innovation—let's look at areas where similar ideas have worked better.

Financial markets: After the Great Depression, we created the Securities and Exchange Commission to sort of police corporate books and make sure this is working.

We have the FASB, the Federal Accounting Standards Board, which is not a government agency, but a public-private partnership of all the various stakeholders, the academics, the consumers, the CFOs, the Big Three or Four accounting firms—I don't remember how many are left—to basically come up with promulgating standards and metrics on accounting which innovate with the time. And if you cook the books and don't follow the standards, the SEC comes and gets you with government enforcement.

So what I am proposing is taking AHRQ, taking it outside of CMS, using it as a stand-alone agency, calling it the Health Care Services Commission, to also set up a board of standards of all the stakeholders, so that you have a standard-setting agency that designs the metrics. But it is the market designing it, more or less with the enforcement mechanism of a health care SEC, if you cook the books.

So when we are designing best practices on how to replace a hip, it is the College of Orthopedic Surgeons that are in the room helping design those standards as technology continues to innovate. So when we are designing metrics on how to measure price on per episode of care, on what does the entire bypass surgery cost, you have got the hospitals in the room saying, here is how we ought to do it. When you are talking about quality standards, you have the actual specialist in the room saying, here is the best way to risk adjust, putting a drug-coated stent versus a non-drug-coated stent; you have the cardiologist doing that.

The point I am trying to make is, this industry innovates very quickly. Health care innovates very fast, faster than government can possibly promulgate regulations. So why not have a system like we have for the financial services sector, which innovates with that sector, in health care, where you have the government saying, if you cook the books, if you deviate, you are going to be penalized. But you have the industry itself, along with consumers, along with all the various stakeholders, government included, designing the metrics on price, designing the metrics on quality, designing the metrics on best practices, putting them out on an apples-to-apples basis, standard metrics, so the market can respond, so consumers can see, so people can shop for value, so employers can reward outcomes, so the payers can actually see what they are getting for their money.

Is that not a better model going forward, than having CMS dictate the terms of all of this stuff, and penalize or reward providers based on what CMS thinks is the best way to practice medicine?

I will start with Peter and go down the road. Would you care to respond to that notion?

Mr. ORSZAG. Do I have an option?

No, I didn't think so. Why don't I phrase it this way?

In the current structure of our public health insurance programs, Medicare and Medicaid, there are decisions that the government needs to reach on what should be reimbursed and what have you. So in a sense you are asking a far larger question about the structure of those programs.

But given those programs, structured roughly like they are, there is a further question which is, can the decision-making process be improved through which reimbursement rates and what-have-you are set? And I think, on that, Dr. Lambrew mentioned—and I know it has come up on the Senate side during hearings—this idea of trying to create some other structure that takes many more of the decisions away from the Ways and Means and Finance Committees and puts them in a Federal Reserve-like structure, both for technical competence and for political insulation.

I would say that CBO will be doing a report on options for that kind of Federal health board which should be out later this year.

Mr. RYAN. All right.

Jeanne?

Ms. LAMBREW. I think there are a lot of analogies with what I discussed and what you just said, and I am excited to have this discussion.

I would say the question becomes how much you want to separate out what I will call "the standard generation" from its use. And I think that what I described here—and I work with with Senator Daschle, who has been thinking a lot about this idea—what we both are thinking is, you would create the standard-setting board with experts—doctors, economists, people who are pure experts—to figure out: is there strong evidence that something is high value or low value? Is there real evidence on trade-offs, whether this one has a marginal impact on quality, but this has an impact on cost? Real trade-offs. Or is there no real evidence, so we have to basically let other people figure out what to do with this?

So our idea is, you have one body create the standards. Then you have other people, because when you start figuring out resources and price, that gets into value judgments, societal judgments, political judgments. So we would separate out the standard development from the use of it.

What I propose in my testimony is, we basically allow MedPAC and the board of trustees for Medicare and other public programs, for example, to use that information, in a devolved way, to act, so it doesn't have to be decided by the Ways and Means Committee and the Energy and Commerce Committee. You basically say, here are the standards, here are your experts who say how to employ that, and then let Medicare do that without the process of coming to Congress every single time.

I think it has to be kind of a trade-off, because having the standard-setting board also say, here is an aggressive way to pay for it, may be, probably, a different set of expertise. That is why we separate them out.

But there are many different models for how you allocate these functions, with the bottom line being—and I firmly agree with this—we need to find a new way for decision-making processes in health policy and trying to move it into the sort of processes I set forward.

Mr. RYAN. We definitely want to get to the same place. That is pretty clear.

Just from being jaded, being in the middle of the committee that oversees this stuff and seeing how politicized this gets, how slow the bureaucracy moves, it is a cautionary tale of how to proceed going forward.

Dr. Gratzer.

Dr. GRATZER. I know that you have drawn heavily in your thinking from the work of Professor Regina Herzlinger, who does talk about a Securities and Exchange Commission for health care. I have enormous respect for Professor Herzlinger. As you know, she also has an affiliation with the Manhattan Institute, and I think she has written probably the second best book on health care to be published in the last half decade.

I am not quite as bullish on all aspects of this as perhaps she is.

Undoubtedly, we have an issue with transparency. We can talk about pricing; that is the tip of the iceberg. We are not just interested in how much each orthopedic surgeon charges. We are interested in how good are they at it.

Mr. RYAN. Without the quality, you can't get the value established.

Dr. GRATZER. Well, a starting point is to look at pricing, because one finds extraordinary things when one looks at that alone. It is very difficult to get pricing. As you know, the Bush White House has attempted to do that, and different people have been approached. And the hospital industry argues that they don't actually have prices, it is the insurance industry; and the insurance industry argues it is the hospital industry.

We know also there have been some experiments with legislation, like in California where hospitals are required to release all their pricing information; and unfortunately, most of what they release is nonsense because they don't really expect to receive the list pricing. So one hears there that blood testing can be $300 at a hospital, but they don't actually get that. Certainly they don't get that from Medicare or Medi-Cal, and they don't get that from the private sector.

So some sort of fair play organization, modeled after the SEC, where you would have more information on pricing, more disclosure of complication rates and low-hanging fruit we can all agree on. I think that might be reasonable.

I am hesitant in pushing forward and saying that such a body could then turn around and identify best practices and so on. I am worried about the politicization that would come from it. I am worried also about other things.

That is not to say that I don't think there is an enormous role for the Federal Government in facilitating information. Let me give you an example, as a practicing psychiatrist.

There are new drugs coming to the market all the time. I treat schizophrenic patients. What is the best antipsychotic? There is no drug company that is going to fund a head-to-head comparison with another on-patent drug. NIMH funded a beautiful study done by psychiatrists at different centers, called CATIE, that gives you great information. Those are the sorts of initiatives I think the Federal Government could do and the sort of research that NIMH and NIH could do.

Again, I am just a little bit hesitant in how much further you want to push. You suggest bringing in the experts and bringing in the orthopods and discussing what are best practices.

But, you know, they do actually have clinical guidelines come out of those bodies. I am not sure there is as much discrepancy in terms of best practices as some would suggest, or that there is as much a role for the Federal Government as some would advocate.

Mr. RYAN. Dr. Gratzer, you practice both in Canada and the U.S., correct?

Dr. GRATZER. Now I am not practicing in the United States.

Mr. RYAN. You practiced in Canada; is that correct?

Dr. GRATZER. That is correct.

Mr. RYAN. I want to ask you one final question.

In the year 2000, the World Health Organization said the French health care system was the best health system in the world. The next year, France declared the system bankrupt.

President Sarkozy now—he won his election on many issues, chief among them saying people are going to have to pay more for their health care expenses out of pocket.

Give us just your top few ideas on lessons learned from the Canadian system and lessons we ought to learn before we overhaul our system, and what we ought to avoid going forward, so that we can learn from your experience and the mistakes that may have been made in Canada, rather than repeating them.

Dr. GRATZER. Sure.

The WHO study is often cited. I fear it is probably not worth the paper it is written on. International comparisons are enormously difficult to do. If you actually look at their data set—and it has been some time since I looked at it—they put a huge emphasis on things like equity and relatively little emphasis on things like timeliness of care.

I would point out that the United States and—for that matter, Canada—finished behind Morocco and Colombia, and I don't think the experts at the WHO, as august and intelligent as they are, really pack their kids up in the morning if they have a cough and fly them to Bogota for care. So I think one has to be enormously cautious about international comparisons.

I think if you look right across the Western world and not just at Canada, as you suggested—the country of my birth—but France and Sweden and Great Britain, you find that these countries are dealing with similar things that we are dealing with right here in the United States, an aging population, the full impact of the high-tech, high-expense medical revolution, the fact that value doesn't necessarily come with higher expenses.

I would also suggest to you that many of those countries, countries with public systems that some in the United States seem to idolize, we see that they haven't found a cure-all. Which isn't to say that there aren't ideas there that are relevant in the United States or there aren't things that we could learn about, for instance, information technology. But in the overall scheme of things, often what they have ended up doing is simply rationing care.

If you see a doctor in Canada or Britain or Sweden, I don't think they have access to the best practices much more than in the United States or other countries. And I think part of the way they have saved money—and let's emphasize those systems are much less expensive than the American system as a percent of GDP—people just have much less access to care.

There is a news item in The Globe and Mail, which is a major newspaper in Canada, kind of like I suppose The New York Times is in the United States. They are talking about a town in Newfoundland, Gander, where they have an annual lottery, and the people who win the lottery get access to the family doctor.

Again, I want to emphasize, there are things we can learn right across the board from these countries, but there is no country we can point to and say, they have gotten everything right and we just need to plagiarize.

Mr. ORSZAG. Could I make a very quick point? I would urge that we dial down a bit the cross-country comparisons, and dial way up the comparisons across parts of the United States. There is so much variation within the United States, within a single payment system under Medicare, where I think we could be learning a lot about ways of improving efficiency.

And the cross-country comparisons are useful for some purposes, but there are lots of problems associated with them. They get way more than attention than the regional variation within the United States, and I think we should try to flip that on its head.

Mr. RYAN. What is helpful with cross-country is policy design decisions.

I think you are right, what is helpful is—look at Louisiana—I think their prices are twice or three times what we have in Wisconsin; you factor utilization in and exempt out for that, it is still a huge, huge delta.

And that is why—correct me if I am wrong, Peter, Dr. Orszag—IT is a big deal, IT and best practices, and seeing very clearly what value you get and then rewarding based on outcomes.

I think we all agree, that is clearly the way to go after where a lot of the waste is in the system. Is that not your point?

Mr. ORSZAG. I think there is substantial inefficiency, and one of the key ways of capturing it is to have a more expansive health IT system that is then used for that purpose.

Ms. LAMBREW. Just a quick note. Thinking about Medicare, we do have significant variations in Medicare when you can argue there shouldn't be that much. But it is still less than what we see more generally, and part of the reason is that providers operate in local contexts. So you know from Wisconsin that your private payers and your Medicare payers generally have lower prices and lower costs than other areas of the country.

This is why I think we have to go beyond doing solutions one program by one program, figure out how to develop a standard, figure out a system to transmit those standards to all parts of the system, public and private; and then—and I think we can't underscore this enough—come in with financial tools, systems to make it the priority, because just having the information out there isn't sufficient.

Chairman SPRATT [presiding]. Thank you very much.

Mr. Becerra.

Mr. BECERRA. Thank you, Mr. Chairman, and thank you to the panelists for their testimony.

Dr. Orszag, a quick question. You mentioned the $700 billion that doesn't seem to get us anything more than we already had. That seems to indicate that we have quite a bit of room to make improvements and dollars to use to make the system much more efficient and successful in its outcomes towards America's health care.

Mr. ORSZAG. I think there are huge opportunities for improving efficiency. The difficulty is how to capture that opportunity.

Mr. BECERRA. If we could capture it, that is $700 billion we could put into the system in more efficient ways.

Mr. ORSZAG. Yes. It is a lot of money, but a big "if."

Mr. BECERRA. They are both big, both big.

Dr. Gratzer, a question for you: I don't think anyone disagrees with you with regard to trying to move towards a health system that places the decisions closer to the home, to the family, to provide them that choice.

The difficulty I think I would have with what you say is that chances are your family, my family, would have far better choices than, say, most of the folks who live in my congressional district in the city of Los Angeles.

The average income in my district, the median income of a family in my district is about $34,000. That is probably about what I make in 3 or 4 months as a Member of Congress, and I guarantee it is probably somewhere around what you make—maybe you make more than I do, as a physician as well. But I think it would be very difficult for a lot of these families to have the choice that your wife had with regard to her back surgery. That is what makes it difficult. They would love to have that choice, to stay closer to home. The problem becomes affordability.

So what Mr. Ryan was saying, and I think what you were saying with regard to the markets—and I am not sure if I would want to use the markets necessarily these days to try to talk about a better role model for our health care. If you look at the financial markets recently, the ups and downs, they would probably cause quite a bit for chaos for health care if people had to depend on a pure market-based system.

Supply and demand works well if it is a pure system. But if your wife demands surgery for her back, if my wife demands surgery for her back, we probably can find it and find a good physician to provide that surgery. I doubt that most of the people who live in my congressional district could make that demand and follow through.

So supply and demand is great so long as, on the demand side, you have the ability to follow through.

At the same time, there is the issue of choice. You are a physician, your wife is a physician, my wife is a physician. I will bet if I told you to make sure that your wife didn't have to go to the hospital to get that surgery in July, you would understand why I was saying that.

My wife and a lot of her colleagues always joke and say, if you are ever going to become seriously ill or injured, make sure it is not in July, because you don't want to go into a hospital in July. Why? That is when most medical students who graduated start their residency program in teaching hospitals or in hospitals that take residents.

So the last thing you want is to be severely injured or ill and have to go to the hospital and the person who is treating you firsthand is a resident, a first-year resident.

I suspect you have probably admonished people the way my wife has admonished me and others that, if you are going to see a physician, make sure the physician you are going to see is board certified. I have got some 20 years of education under my belt, 4 as undergraduate, 3 as a law student. I wouldn't have known to ask that M.D., by the way, are you board certified in that particular field? But now I do because I happen to have a physician as a spouse who says to me, make sure that physician you are going to see is board certified.

These are all choices we get to make, but some people have better information than others do, and some have a better ability to make choices and make the demands than others do. And so I think if we could figure out how to make better use of the $700 billion that is out there and then be able to give everyone in America, including those 47 million Americans who don't have health insurance, a choice so they can make a demand, to make sure the supply meets the demand, then I think we would be there. But at this stage we still have so many people who don't have even basic access to health insurance that the choice your wife gets to make, my wife gets to make, that we get to make is not yet there.

And I thank all of you for your testimony. I don't really have a question, but I think it is important to note that there are good ideas out there. It is just a matter of making sure that we match the good ideas to the good intentions to make sure everyone in America can make good use of those ideas.

Mr. Chairman, I yield back the balance of my time; and I thank the panel for their time as well.

Chairman SPRATT. Thank you, Mr. Becerra.

Mr. Smith.

Mr. SMITH. Thank you, Mr. Chairman.

I guess, Dr. Gratzer, if you wouldn't mind, what is the availability of information? Let's just say, most basic, for a patient wishing to know how much a procedure will cost before they undergo the procedure, can they call? What is the likelihood of being able to find out the cost before it is done?

Dr. GRATZER. That is a surprisingly complicated question. If you asked me what is the price of a Toyota Camry in different places in the United States, it is a pretty easy question to answer. It is very difficult for individuals to get pricing information.

Now, again, it depends if they are in the public sector or the private sector in terms of their insurance. As you know, HHS has been trying to release more data.

As you know, different companies like Aetna and so on have experimented with better disclosure of how much, say, specialists in Cincinnati are compensated for consults. But, for the most part, it is very difficult to get that sort of information available. Which I think also suggests some of the enormous problems that people who champion consumer driven health care face, because there is not that much consumerism to be had if you don't have good information available.

So I think wherever you sit on this debate, though, one can appreciate that we need more information, both on pricing and, ultimately, on pricing and quality.

Ms. LAMBREW. I think that we need to be careful about more versus better. Because the reality is that we do have a fair amount of information on things that we potentially can't use. In fact, there has been some studies that are interesting that say sometimes there is too much information for effective decision making. The classic study being that if you give people many, many choices of ice cream they choose chocolate, vanilla and strawberry, versus you give them 10 choices they can digest them and choose across a broader range of that.

So I think that we need to look at the type of information that people should have. People want to know the information on their doctor so they can make a choice to a degree. I think it is always a little bit more about word of mouth and other factors, but they want to choose their doctors, they want information on their plans, and then they want information at the point of service when there is a real choice.

I think we need to figure out how to structure the information around those types of choices so it is useful, effective and promotes high value, and take some of the other information, when there is a clearly effective service or a clearly better way to deliver health care, to adopt it. Because we can't reduce that variation without at some point saying, this does work. Let's use every tool that we have to promote it.

Mr. ORSZAG. Can I just add two quick points?

In the written testimony, there is a little discussion of this.

I think there are two things to remember about the price transparency for individual transactions, for medical services, this surgery, that surgery, et cetera. First is such a large share of health costs are insured, something like 80 percent or so, which obviously diminishes the incentive to kind of shop around, if you will.

And then, secondly, that many health care markets are local, and many of those local health care markets are quite concentrated. And evidence from other sectors suggests when there is more price transparency with that kind of industrial organization setting, where there is only a limited number of competitors, basically, the effect can be to facilitate collusion. So if you are thinking about two hospitals in an area and you start publicizing prices for individual transactions, the effect in other sectors has been not to reduce the average price but to increase it because of collusion.

Mr. SMITH. So there is evidence that through more disclosure of price that that leads to price fixing or a collusion?

Mr. ORSZAG. Yes, there is. And so that would be a concern that would need to be very carefully attended to with more price transparency in local health markets.

Mr. SMITH. So I guess what I am getting at is what is the incidence of a patient needing to pay for an office call with the provider before they know how much it is going to cost?

Mr. ORSZAG. Oh, I am not denying there is very little transparency that exists currently in terms of how much things actually cost. If you were quoted a price, that, as was already mentioned, is often not the final price but rather just a starting point for negotiation anyway.

But the question I was trying to answer is what if we had a lot more transparency about the underlying cost or price of the doctor visit or the MRI or the surgery. And I think in our heads we all think that will lead to significant reductions in cost because we will be a bunch of very savvy consumers shopping around. And there is a limit to the degree to which that will happen to the extent you are insured and therefore don't have much incentive to shop around, first.

And then, secondly—and that's on the beneficiary side. And on the provider side you could be facilitating collusion and moving towards more monopoly pricing, rather than competitive pricing, which is just a concern that would need to be again sort of very carefully monitored by antitrust and other authorities.

Mr. SMITH. Absolutely. I would speculate that it would be easier to detect collusion with more information available to the public, getting more people chatting about it and perhaps—I mean, there will always be that risk with more information, but, to me, it would be a greater opportunity for detection.

Mr. ORSZAG. Let me just pin in, focus in on that. What you would expect with more transparency is that, currently, there is some distribution of prices basically, and that it would collapse. It would—you know, there would be much less variance in the prices. But whether that collapses to a higher or lower average price depends on the provider behavior in addition to beneficiary behavior, and that is where it can get a little dicey.

We put out a policy brief on this topic a few months ago which I will get to you with examples of other sectors where this has actually led to higher rather than lower prices.

[The information follows:]

ECONOMIC AND BUDGET ISSUE BRIEF

CBO

A series of issue summaries from the Congressional Budget Office

JUNE 5, 2008

Increasing Transparency in the Pricing of Health Care Services and Pharmaceuticals

The rising cost of health care represents the nation's single most important long-term fiscal challenge. This brief explores whether increased transparency about prices for specific health care services and pharmaceuticals would help to temper the rapid growth in costs. The answer is unclear because evidence can be marshaled on both sides of the issue.

Some observers believe that if individuals know the prices of health care services, they are more likely to seek out less expensive providers or treatments and to question how effective the care they are purchasing is likely to be.

But several factors may limit the effectiveness of this type of transparency in cutting health care expenditures. On the consumer side, more than 80 percent of the population is covered by some form of health insurance, which insulates people from the full price of the health care they consume, limiting their incentive to compare prices. Doctors and other health professionals often direct decisions about what services to buy from whom, as individuals may have little information on the care they need or the quality or value of that care. Moreover, for insured and uninsured people alike, awareness of prices will make little difference in emergency situations or in the relatively small number of cases that account for a disproportionate share of overall health care spending.

On the provider side, more transparency would make information about the prices that hospitals, physicians, and drug companies charge insurers more visible, but whether such disclosure would lead to higher or lower prices for consumers on average is unclear and depends on the nature of competition in the relevant market. The markets for some health care services are highly concentrated, so increasing transparency in such markets could lead to higher, rather than lower, prices because higher prices are easier to maintain when the prices charged by each provider involved can be observed by all of the others. Whatever the effect on average prices, more transparent prices would probably reduce the range of prices.

Questions about transparency in health care costs extend beyond the prices for specific services and pharmaceuticals. Workers pay for employment-based health insurance through reduced take-home pay, but those costs may not be evident to many of them. A greater awareness of the total costs of health care and who ultimately bears them might generate increased demand for efficiency in that sector.

What Is Price Transparency?

The price of a particular health care service is not uniform among providers or payers. Although a provider may have a list price for a particular service, the actual transaction price for that service varies widely, depending on the type of payer—individuals, governments, or insurance companies. Moreover, competing providers may collect different payments from different payers or types of payers. Therefore, in health care markets, list prices are often higher than what the provider accepts as payment in full from a particular payer.

With so many different prices applicable to a particular health care service, it is perhaps not surprising that a consistent definition of the term "price transparency" is elusive. Publication of list prices has at times been referred to as transparency, but the term could also be used to describe insurers' efforts to make available to their subscribers the rates that they have negotiated with physicians and hospitals. A more expansive definition of transparency would make those rates available to anyone and not limit them to subscribers. Alternatively, a government agency or other entity could report average prices. Certainly, those different concepts of transparency may elicit different responses from consumers and providers.

Who Buys and Sells Health Care and at What Prices?

There are three primary payers for health care: individuals, governments, and private insurers. When an individual decides to seek care, in most cases payments from government insurance, such as Medicare or Medicaid, or from a private health insurer supplement the person's out-of-pocket spending. The 16 percent of individuals who lack health insurance face all of the charges for the health care they receive, though some may receive uncompensated care (either as charity or as a debt written off by the provider), reducing their out-of-pocket spending.

Health care providers are on the other side of that transaction. There are many types of providers: hospitals, physicians, pharmaceutical companies, laboratories, imaging centers for such services as MRIs (magnetic resonance images) and X-rays, physical therapists, nursing homes, and others. This brief focuses on the three largest components of health care spending—hospital care, services by physicians, and prescription drugs—which together accounted for about two-thirds of national health expenditures in 2006.[1]

For each good or service it delivers, a hospital or physician practice may bill a patient (or his or her insurer) according to its list prices. However, most patients' accounts are settled for a smaller amount, with the actual transaction price depending on the individual's insurance arrangement.[2] The rates for Medicare and Medicaid patients are set unilaterally by the federal and state governments, respectively, and are frequently publicly available.[3] Those payments are typically lower than the rates providers accept from private health insurers, with Medicare's generally exceeding Medicaid's.

For an individual with commercial health insurance, the price a provider typically accepts as payment in full is the result of a contract negotiated between the insurer and the provider. Such contracts usually require that the prices they set be kept confidential. Some insurers are beginning to make many of those prices accessible to their subscribers, which may make confidentiality more difficult to maintain. For prescription drugs, the system of charges and rebates that determines final prices to consumers and their insurers is particularly complex.[4]

An individual without insurance or someone whose insurance company has not reached an agreement with a provider is usually responsible for paying the provider's list price. Such prices are not usually bound by the confidentiality that governs the prices negotiated between providers and health plans, but they may still not be accessible or comprehensible to people.

What Information on Prices Is Available?

State governments, state-level industry associations, and various private organizations have started to publish prices for some health care services, usually hospital services. The usefulness of that information to individuals is likely to vary, both with the type of service they require (emergency care as opposed to treatment planned in advance) and with their health insurance status.

Programs in Wisconsin and California present information that is typical of that offered by many state governments and industry associations.[5] The Wisconsin

1. Department of Health and Human Services, Centers for Medicare and Medicaid Services, National Health Expenditure data, January 8, 2008.

2. Hospitals in Maryland are an exception. The state requires the same price for all payers. See Maryland Health Services Cost Review Commission, *Maryland Hospital Pricing Guide* (December 2006).

3. Although Medicare's and Medicaid's payment rates are public, they are typically set using coding systems and formulas that may not be easily understood by the average patient. For Medicare's fee schedules, see www.cms.hhs.gov/FeeScheduleGenInfo or www.cms.hhs.gov/ProspMedicareFeeSvcPmtGen. Medicaid's fee schedules differ by state. See, for example, Wisconsin's: dhfs.wisconsin.gov/medicaid4/maxfees/maxfee.htm.

4. See Congressional Budget Office, *Prescription Drug Pricing in the Private Sector* (January 2007).

5. See the Wisconsin PricePoint System, available at www.wipricepoint.org. See also the Web site of California's Office of Statewide Health Planning and Development, www.oshpd.ca.gov/HID/Products/Hospitals/Chrgmstr/index.html.

Hospital Association collects information from its members on their average and median charges to patients for a number of procedures. Since 2005, California has required hospitals to submit to the state and to make available to patients a copy of their list prices for all goods and services. Such information may be of only limited usefulness to people, though. The information made available in Wisconsin and California includes only hospitals' charges and so leaves out other important charges. Perhaps the most important exclusion is the price of the services provided by physicians—surgeons, anesthesiologists, and others—during a hospital stay. In addition, individuals with health insurance coverage may face very different total prices and out-of-pocket expenses if their insurer has negotiated discounted rates. Rankings based on list prices may not hold for the prices insurers have negotiated.

A New Hampshire initiative includes some of the information that others omit. The state's Insurance Department collects detailed information from insurance claims data and, for each of the state's largest health insurers, reports estimates of total prices and out-of-pocket expenses for an entire episode of care, including the prices paid for physicians' services.[6]

The private sector is also reporting data on the price of hospital care, an indication that some firms believe consumers will value comparison shopping for health care. Those private ventures are more varied, and each example takes a different approach. Vimo, a private firm that provides information about health insurance providers, reports both a hospital's list prices for procedures and its own estimate of the range of negotiated rates the hospital has agreed to with insurers. In Minnesota, Carol, another private firm, reports list prices from health care providers that have paid a fee to participate. However, those list prices are for provider-designed bundles of services that may not match insurers' coverage or be easily compared. Insurers have also begun to provide pricing information to their subscribers.[7]

6. See New Hampshire's HealthCost Web site, www.nhhealthcost.org.

7. For details on two instances, see www.aetna.com/news/2007/1003.htm and www.humana.com/members/tools/transparency.asp.

What Are the Potential Benefits of Price Transparency?

The primary argument in favor of more transparent pricing for specific health care services is that better information on prices will lead consumers to use health care more efficiently.[8] For some individuals, the information could allow them to consider various providers to find the one offering the lowest price. Other people may opt not to seek care for a particular ailment, deciding that their condition is not serious enough to warrant the expense or that the promise of a remedy is not likely enough to justify the price of treatment. Still others may use the information to compare the prices of alternative treatments—a course of physical therapy versus surgery, for example.

People who do not have health insurance and those whose insurance arrangements require substantial out-of-pocket expenditures through large deductibles or other cost sharing are more likely to adjust their health care spending in response to prices. In particular, individuals enrolled in consumer-directed health plans, which combine a high-deductible insurance policy with tax-sheltered accounts to finance out-of-pocket payments, would probably find price transparency more useful than individuals with policies involving HMOs (health maintenance organizations) or PPOs (preferred provider organizations), for which cost sharing may involve only a fixed-dollar copayment.[9] Although enrollment in those high-deductible policies has been growing since health reimbursement accounts (HRAs) and health savings accounts (HSAs) were approved in 2002 and 2003, respectively, those plans still represent a small share of the market. According to the Congressional Budget Office's (CBO's) estimates, by January 2006, approximately 6 million people were enrolled in insurance policies eligible for HRAs or HSAs, compared with the 180 million people under age 65 who had private health insurance coverage that year.[10]

8. See the statement of Regina E. Herzlinger, Professor of Business Administration, Harvard Business School, before the Subcommittee on Health of the House Committee on Ways and Means (July 18, 2006).

9. Once an individual's health care spending exceeds that high deductible, the incentive to shop on the basis of price falls.

10. Congressional Budget Office, *Consumer-Directed Health Plans: Potential Effects on Health Care Spending and Outcomes* (December 2006), p. xi; and U.S. Census Bureau, *Income, Poverty, and Health Insurance Coverage in the United States: 2006* (August 2007), Table C-3.

For people with a greater degree of cost sharing in their health insurance plans, more transparent pricing might reduce their consumption of health care or redirect it to less costly choices. The RAND Health Insurance Experiment, conducted in the 1970s and 1980s, showed that individuals purchase less health care when faced with greater cost sharing and that the reduction in health care services had little impact on their health.[11] Although that study did not consider the question of price transparency, its results suggest that individuals who pay for health care on their own are responsive to out-of-pocket payments. At the same time, the evidence indicated that the primary effect was on whether individuals sought care for a medical condition; once they went to a doctor, subsequent spending per person was similar in the different cost-sharing arrangements.

Researchers have studied the effects of price transparency in markets outside of health care and found that individuals alter their purchasing behavior when there is a change in the price transparency of a good they already consume and for which they pay the full price. For example, in one study, drivers in the United States were more likely to cut their use of toll roads when the price of a cash toll was posted than when the road had an electronic transponder toll payment system like E-ZPass, which might not quote the price of an individual toll.[12] Experiments with real-time pricing of electricity showed that French retail customers shifted their use from higher- to lower-priced time periods.[13]

However, consumption of specific health care services might not show a similar response to more transparent pricing. Insured individuals generally pay only a portion of the total price and may not understand their payment responsibilities, so their behavior might not match that of consumers who face the full price of a good.[14] In some instances, moreover, there may be only one reliable course of treatment available. Finally, many purchases of health care cannot be planned ahead of time and shifted to lower-priced providers; in an emergency, people generally will go to the nearest available provider.

What Are the Potential Disadvantages of Price Transparency?

The markets for some health care services are highly concentrated, and increasing transparency in such markets could lead to higher, rather than lower, prices. In markets where only a small number of firms operate, increased transparency would make it easier for those firms to observe the prices charged by their rivals, which could lead to reduced competition between them. In health care, reduced competition might result if more transparent pricing revealed the prices negotiated between insurers and providers, especially in concentrated markets.

What Factors Might Lead to Higher Prices?

For the most part, the market for health care services is local. An individual choosing a physician or a hospital for care will, in general, be choosing among local providers, who may compete with one another.[15] The degree of competition varies a great deal from one market to the next within the United States. Within a local area, the competitive landscape is also likely to differ across types of providers. For example, in a city with only one or two hospitals, there may still be extensive competition among many primary care physicians.[16]

More concentrated markets with fewer sellers are more likely to be conducive to the sort of coordination that would produce higher prices.[17] In those instances, price

11. Willard G. Manning and others, "Health Insurance and the Demand for Medical Care: Evidence from a Randomized Experiment," *American Economic Review*, vol. 77, no. 3 (June 1987), pp. 251–277.

12. Amy Finkelstein, "E-ZTax: Tax Salience and Tax Rates," Working Paper No. 12924 (Cambridge, Mass., National Bureau of Economic Research, February 2007).

13. Christophe Aubin and others, "Real-Time Pricing of Electricity of Residential Customers: Econometric Analysis of an Experiment," *Journal of Applied Econometrics*, vol. 10, no. S1 (November 2006), pp. S171–S191.

14. LASIK (laser-assisted in situ keratomileusis), cosmetic surgery, and dental care are not typically covered by insurance, but one study investigating price comparison shopping for them found limited to no shopping on that basis for those services, largely because of concerns about quality; referrals were more important. See Ha T. Tu and Jessica May, "Self-Pay Markets in Health Care: Consumer Nirvana or Caveat Emptor?" *Health Affairs*, Web Exclusive, vol. 26, no. 2 (February 6, 2007), pp. w217–w226.

15. Exceptions include patients who have unusual illnesses or who travel to a marquee clinic or physician for treatment.

16. However, the level of competition in the hospital market is likely to have an impact on the level of competition in services by physicians, because any physician entering the market will typically seek privileges at one of the local hospitals.

17. See Organisation for Economic Co-operation and Development, Directorate for Financial, Fiscal, and Enterprise Affairs, Committee on Competition Law and Policy, "Price Transparency," September 11, 2001.

transparency makes it easy to observe a competitor's prices and to respond to them. The incentive to price aggressively is reduced because a firm considering offering a lower price to gain more business knows that its few competitors could quickly observe that action and cut their prices to deny the firm its advantage or even to punish the firm.

Although economists might agree about the potential for such effects to arise, there is little empirical evidence about their extent. Studies of laws requiring greater transparency in other concentrated industries suggest that more transparency resulted in higher prices. Two studies have examined a change in a U.S. law in the late 1980s that required railroads to disclose some of their contract terms with grain shippers. One found that rail rates increased once the requirement took effect.[18] The other study found that rail rates rose on routes without water competition but fell on routes where barges could more easily substitute.[19] Thus, both studies suggest that railroads took advantage of the requirement for transparency to raise rates when they could observe what their competitors in concentrated markets were charging. Subsequent researchers, however, have raised concerns about the reliability of the data the studies used.[20]

A study of the Danish concrete industry that examined prices following the antitrust authority's decision to publish firms' transaction prices receives frequent mention in any discussion of increasing price transparency. The authors found that the average price of concrete rose between 15 percent and 20 percent following the publication of prices and concluded that the dissemination of price information empowered firms to practice tacit collusion.[21] Observing their rivals' prices made it possible for firms to charge higher prices without fear of being underbid. However, that result was based on a small sample of plants over a short period.

Hospital Markets. Hospital markets in the United States have grown steadily more concentrated, leaving some hospitals with the potential for substantial market power. One study counts an average of 58 consolidations each year between 1990 and 2003 in the United States.[22] Even without transparency, as a local market grows more concentrated, its hospitals or hospital systems may gain the power to demand higher payment rates from insurers simply because there are fewer choices. Alternatively, some consolidations could produce economies of scale or scope that lower the costs to supply care. The type of hospital seems not to matter, as studies indicate that the pricing behavior and consolidation patterns for nonprofit hospitals are similar to those of for-profit hospitals.[23]

Even when they do not know the precise rates at which competitors are paid, hospitals may press for higher rates to be more in line with their competition. One study recounts that an effort by Blue Cross of California to convey information about hospital prices to its PPO enrollees by marking the lowest-priced hospitals with "$" and the highest-priced with "$$$$" was halted in part because so many low-priced hospitals pushed for higher prices.[24] It is not clear, however, whether that pressure was the result simply of efforts to seek greater profits or a reaction out of fear that being pegged as low-priced would also suggest low-quality care.

Physician Markets. The markets for physicians' services are often far less concentrated than hospital markets, reducing the likelihood that greater transparency would lead to higher prices. Though entry to the market is certainly expensive (training, licensing, and establishing a practice are all costly), the barriers are much lower than

18. Stephen W. Fuller, Fred J. Ruppel, and David A. Bessler, "Effect of Contract Disclosure on Price: Railroad Grain Contracting in the Plains," *Western Journal of Agricultural Economics*, vol. 15, no. 2 (December 1990), pp. 265–271.

19. John Schmitz and Stephen W. Fuller, "Effect of Contract Disclosure on Railroad Grain Rates: An Analysis of Corn Belt Corridors," *Logistics and Transportation Review*, vol. 31, no. 2 (June 1995), pp. 97–124.

20. K. Eric Wolfe and William P. Linde, "The Carload Waybill Statistics: Usefulness for Economic Analysis," *Journal of the Transportation Research Forum*, vol. 36, no. 2 (1997), pp. 26–41.

21. Svend Albaek, Peter Mollgaard, and Per B. Overgaard, "Government-Assisted Oligopoly Coordination? A Concrete Case," *Journal of Industrial Economics*, vol. 45, no. 4 (December 1997), pp. 429–443.

22. Robert Town and others, "The Welfare Consequences of Hospital Mergers," Working Paper No. 12244 (Cambridge, Mass.: National Bureau of Economic Research, May 2006).

23. See Congressional Budget Office, *Nonprofit Hospitals and the Provision of Community Benefits* (December 2006); and John Carreyrou and Barbara Martinez, "Nonprofit Hospitals, Once for the Poor, Strike It Rich," *Wall Street Journal*, April 4, 2008, p. A1.

24. Paul B. Ginsburg, "Shopping for Price in Medical Care," *Health Affairs*, Web Exclusive, vol. 26, no. 2 (February 6, 2007), p. w213.

for hospitals. Except in some specialty markets, individual physicians therefore have little or no market power to exercise in their negotiations with health insurers. In fact, there have been numerous cases of physicians working together, allegedly anticompetitively, to obtain better contract terms from insurers, and of insurers agreeing to preferential rates for sizable local groups of physicians.[25] With so many competitors to observe, individual physicians would be less likely than hospitals to be able to use more transparent pricing successfully to demand higher payments from health insurers. Conversely, a lack of price transparency can be a problem for physicians because it leaves them unsure of the payment amount they can expect for a service.

Prescription Drug Markets. Spending on prescription drugs totaled $217 billion in 2006, or 11 percent of health expenditures.[26] Brand-name pharmaceuticals that are sheltered from competition under patent protection may enjoy substantial market power and even monopoly power to the extent that no alternative drugs effectively treat the same condition. Even those drugs with competition from generic alternatives are likely to have only a limited number of rivals. For individuals with prescription drug insurance coverage, the final price that they and their insurer together pay for a prescription drug is significantly influenced by the rebate the manufacturer grants to the health insurer or to the pharmacy benefit manager (PBM) acting as the insurer's agent.[27] The insurer or PBM negotiates those discounts on the basis of a volume of business or a market share that it guarantees for the manufacturer or on the preferred status that it grants to a range of the manufacturer's products. CBO's past work has noted that requiring the disclosure of discounts made to prescription drug plans in the Medicare program could set in place conditions for tacit collusion, as manufacturers would find it more difficult to set prices below their competitors' without detection.[28]

There are a number of different benchmarks for drug prices, but many are based on list prices and do not take into account the discounts and rebates that manufacturers grant insurers and PBMs. In conjunction with a change in the rules governing Medicaid's reimbursement for prescription drugs, the Centers for Medicare and Medicaid Services was to collect and publish what is termed the average manufacturer price (AMP) for prescription drugs starting in 2007, but legal action has delayed the endeavor.[29] Though revealing the AMP would not allow competitors to observe their rivals' prices directly, it could alter the balance of bargaining power between payers and manufacturers in negotiating discounts and move the average price higher or lower.

What Factors Might Prevent Higher Prices?

Though many health care providers have significant market power, they do not operate unchecked. Just as providers attempt to use their market power to press for higher prices, insurers attempt to use their market power to push prices down. In addition to that market discipline, antitrust authorities may intervene if they suspect anticompetitive behavior.

Health Insurers. Insurance—either public or private—is the primary payer for most purchases of health care in the United States. The prices paid by Medicare and Medicaid are set by regulators and are generally publicly available and therefore may serve as a benchmark for negotiations between private insurers and health care providers. With transparency, what happened to those negotiated prices would depend in large part on whether providers or insurers had more bargaining power.

25. See, for example, Federal Trade Commission, "Texas Doctors' IPA Agrees to Settle Price Fixing Charges" (press release, February 13, 2006), available at www.ftc.gov/opa/2006/02/laredo.shtm.

26. Department of Health and Human Services, Centers for Medicare and Medicaid Services, National Health Expenditure data, January 8, 2008.

27. Individuals without insurance coverage for prescription drugs pay the entire retail price themselves, making the price transparent at the point of purchase. There may be substantial variation in prices among pharmacies, though it may be difficult to uncover those differences. See Ha T. Tu and Catherine G. Corey, *State Prescription Drug Price Web Sites: How Useful to Consumers?* Research Brief No. 1 (Washington, D.C.: Center for Studying Health System Change, February 2008).

28. Congressional Budget Office, *Potential Effects of Disclosing Price Rebates on the Medicare Drug Benefit* (March 12, 2007). The Federal Trade Commission expressed similar concerns about an earlier proposal in California that ultimately was not implemented. See the letter from Susan A. Creighton and others, Federal Trade Commission, Bureau of Competition, Bureau of Economics, and Office of Policy Planning, to Greg Aghazarian, California Assembly Member, September 7, 2004.

29. Letter from Gale P. Arden, Director, Center for Medicaid and State Operations, Disabled and Elderly Health Programs Group, to State Medicaid Directors, December 21, 2007, available at www.cms.hhs.gov/DeficitReductionAct/Downloads/SMDAMPLetter.pdf.

Health insurance plans have substantial bargaining power in their negotiations with health care providers. Larger health insurers are able to extract larger discounts from providers, and, like hospital markets, the health insurance market has grown more concentrated.[30] The American Medical Association reports that two large private health insurance companies in the United States—WellPoint Inc. and UnitedHealth Group—now cover 67 million people, or more than one-third of the commercial health insurance market, following numerous acquisitions between 2000 and 2007.[31] Another study found that the largest commercial insurer controlled at least one-third of the market in 38 states and more than half the market in 16 states in 2002 and 2003. The largest three plans controlled more than 50 percent of the market in all but three states.[32] The potential for other health insurers to enter a market may exert some competitive pressure on the existing insurers, but the opportunity for entry may be limited. According to that same analysis, the four largest national health plans (along with regional Blue Cross and Blue Shield plans) already operate in most states, so, in addition to regulatory barriers, new insurers could face difficulties in building networks of providers and subscribers.

Although it is difficult to know how concentration in the health insurance market might alter the effects of transparency, one study has found that that concentration can counteract aspects of concentration in hospital markets.[33] In markets where there was more competition between HMOs—and each one therefore had less market power to exercise in negotiating with hospitals—a hospital merger led to higher health insurance premiums. Where there was little competition between HMOs, however, a hospital merger had no effect on premiums. There, an HMO's market power could counteract the hospitals' increase in market power to prevent higher prices. On the whole, although both markets have grown more concentrated, one analyst concludes that hospitals' bargaining position stands to benefit more from improved transparency than insurers' bargaining position does.[34]

Antitrust Authorities. In an effort to prevent health care firms from coordinating to raise prices, federal antitrust authorities have issued guidelines to describe a "safety zone" for the dissemination of fee information that will be available to competing providers.[35] To stay in the safety zone and avoid scrutiny by antitrust authorities, collective disclosure of fee information must meet three requirements: The information must be collected by a third party, any information that is available to competitors must be at least three months old, and the information must be collected from enough sources so that no individual provider's price may be identified.

That last requirement would seem to prevent the public release of the prices negotiated between providers and insurers, but it does not preclude a provider or an insurer, acting independently, from disclosing those prices to its patients or subscribers. The health insurer Aetna has initiated such a program in a number of the local markets it serves. That level of transparency may be useful to people already enrolled in a health insurance plan to see the possibly different rates charged by each of the providers who participate in their insurer's network. However, it would not help people choose a health insurance plan by allowing them to compare the prices different insurers have negotiated. Though publicly available prices might raise concerns about anticompetitive behavior, they could be useful to the many people choosing among insurance plans and seeking to minimize their total out-of-pocket spending on both insurance and health care.[36]

Aggregated or average price information would make it more difficult for providers to coordinate higher prices because individual providers' prices would not be obvious. That aggregated information might be of limited use to people, because it would not allow comparisons of

30. It is not clear how consolidation of health care plans and hospital systems into national companies has affected the bargaining process. Leverage in one city market could be used to gain better terms in another.

31. American Medical Association, *Competition in Health Insurance: A Comprehensive Study of U.S. Markets, 2007 Update* (2007).

32. James C. Robinson, "Consolidation and the Transformation of Competition in Health Insurance," *Health Affairs*, vol. 23, no. 6 (November/December 2004), pp. 11–24.

33. Town and others, "The Welfare Consequences of Hospital Mergers."

34. Ginsburg, "Shopping for Price in Medical Care," p. w214.

35. See U.S. Department of Justice and Federal Trade Commission. *Statements of Antitrust Enforcement Policy in Health Care*, Statements 5 and 6 (August 1996).

36. Those individuals would include policyholders who purchase coverage in the individual market, employees whose employers offer two or more health insurance plans, and married individuals eligible for coverage through either spouse's employer.

actual prices for different providers and different treatments. In small markets, where there may be fewer than five hospitals or other providers, even providing aggregated information would appear to fall outside the safety zone.

What Could Happen to the Range of Prices Paid?

More transparent prices would probably reduce the range of prices that providers agreed to with payers as the new information altered the balance of bargaining power.[37] That narrowing might happen in two different ways. A given provider might find price discrimination—charging different payers different prices—more difficult. Payers facing the high rates could use more transparent price information to press the provider for lower prices. Meanwhile, those private payers at the low end of the provider's accepted payment range might see prices rise, driven by the provider's ability to observe rivals' prices and the provider's desire to reduce the pressure to lower rates for high-end payers. More transparency would also shrink the range of prices paid by reducing the variation in prices among different providers. With transparency, low-price providers would see the opportunity to raise rates, and high-price providers would seek to avoid losing clients to rivals with lower prices. Such compressing effects would also be expected if providers' average prices were published. As long as there were enough different transactions that averages did not reveal the prices paid by individual payers, concerns about the potential for less aggressive price competition would be attenuated.

As an example, German electricity markets experienced a reduction in price dispersion following the government's requirement that operators of transmission networks publish their access charges. In the year after the change, the average charge was little changed, but the variance decreased.[38] The operators with the lowest prices before the requirement took effect raised their rates, while those with high prices reduced them.

37. For further discussion, see Congressional Budget Office, *Potential Effects of Disclosing Price Rebates*.

38. Christian Growitsch and Thomas Wein, "Negotiated Third Party Access—An Industrial Organisation Perspective," *European Journal of Law and Economics*, vol. 20, no. 3 (2005), pp. 165–183.

What Is the Likely Net Effect of More Price Transparency?

The implications of increased price transparency on the average price of health care goods and services, total health care spending, and the federal budget are ambiguous. The confluence of many factors—changes in individuals' actions, the lack of incentives or feasibility for many individuals to change their behavior in purchasing health care, the potential for less aggressive pricing in markets where providers are concentrated, the counterweight in markets where insurers are concentrated, and the reduced variation in prices—makes it difficult to determine which forces would ultimately outweigh the others. In addition, the interpretation of price transparency used might also influence the end result for average prices and health care spending.

If, for example, insurers have a stronger bargaining position than providers and if enough individuals pay for a substantial portion of their care out of pocket, price transparency that reveals insurers' negotiated rates could bring lower average prices and less spending. Conversely, when providers have a stronger position and individuals have few incentives or little ability to conserve health care spending, that same transparency could produce higher average prices and spending. Those results, however, may hold only in the short term, as health care providers decide to enter or leave health care markets in response to the prices they receive.

This brief was prepared by Sheila Campbell. It and other CBO publications are available at the agency's Web site (www.cbo.gov).

Peter R. Orszag
Director

Mr. SMITH. Okay. Thank you, Mr. Chairman.

Chairman SPRATT. Mr. Doggett.

Mr. DOGGETT. Thank you, Mr. Chairman; and thank you for the testimony that each of you have offered.

Dr. Orszag, if I understand your testimony, it is that we have $700 billion of waste in our health care system and one of our goals is to try to reduce or eliminate that waste.

Mr. ORSZAG. Let me rephrase it carefully. Credible estimates suggest that as much as $700 billion a year is delivered in health care services, surgeries, MRIs, doctor visits that don't improve health outcomes. That is a lot of money.

Mr. DOGGETT. If they don't improve health care outcomes, they are wasteful expenditures.

Mr. ORSZAG. They are wasteful in terms of improving health outcomes. The providers may not view them as wasteful.

Mr. DOGGETT. Well, and that goes to the heart of how we address the problem.

You have also said—and there has been kind of a suggestion among some of these questions—that if we have the truth it will set us free. And I think you have pointed out that just having information, just having disclosure is not a panacea, that in fact it will only add cost to the health care system and be of academic interest unless you link that disclosure specifically to comparative effectiveness and have financial disincentives so that you are not rewarded for waste.

Mr. ORSZAG. I think that's right.

Just to focus on the fact, while I think in general for consumer behavior the Econ 101 perspective is exaggerated, on the provider side, we do need to remember financial incentives matter; and to a first approximation in health care we get what we provide financial incentives for providers to provide. And unless you are going to change the payment methodology, you are not going to wind up with a more efficient health care system.

Mr. DOGGETT. You have also suggested that if you really want to have comprehensive information technology where all health care providers use it, just providing financial incentives will only encourage those who are about to adopt it anyway and that what we need to do, ultimately, is to set a timeline by which if you don't adopt the technology you don't get a penny of government money.

Mr. ORSZAG. Yeah, let me come back to that. Because that had come up earlier.

So one approach is to provide some tax credit or a payment or subsidy for adopting health IT. The problem with that is the folks who already view it as beneficial for their own operations to adopt will have done so, and there will be more of them over time even without Federal intervention.

And so what are you doing? You are flipping those people who were sort of close to the line, who from their own perspective were pretty close. And if you want to keep the fiscal costs contained, you are not going to have a huge subsidy.

I was asked earlier, what else could we do? Well, you know, it is either the carrot or the stick. That is kind of the carrot and then there is the stick approach. In e-prescribing and other approaches, you can combine both of them. You could provide a small subsidy up front during a 3- or 4-year transition and say, thereafter, you won't receive Medicare reimbursement unless you've adopted.

I'd also note that is not a perfect system. The Medicare approach, for example, pediatricians and others who might fall outside of the bulk of the Medicare system may require some other kind of approach.

Mr. DOGGETT. I want to involve Dr. Lambrew in this, also.

If the goal here is just get the government out of the way and turn all of this over to those who have a financial interest in the outcome, let PhRMA decide pharmaceuticals, let some kind of surgeon decide what kind of surgery we will reward, that certainly won't eliminate that $700 billion of waste, will it?

Ms. LAMBREW. I don't think so. I think that, going back to the car analogy, because that is what we usually do in health care——

Mr. DOGGETT. Better than a financial services analogy.

Ms. LAMBREW. Exactly. It is not as though trying to pick a drug or picking a doctor is like buying a car. It is more analogous to trying to say people should be buying the parts for their car and putting it together themselves.

We have to think through systems. We know that thinking through choice of organizations where you get care, because the organizations then have the infrastructure, the multiple specialists, nurses, the other components of a high-functioning health care system matters.

We also know that having somebody help structure the choices for health insurance matters. Employers do these days really make discriminating decisions on behalf of many people to figure out what is a high-value health insurance plan. Unfortunately, there is often not as many choices as they would like. We see a real consolidation of the insurance industry.

I did a study about 5 years ago in which we asked people, which would you rather have, the money your employer pays and go out and buy insurance on your own or a set of a couple of choices, three to five choices of health insurance plans? And, by far, people wanted their employers to help them.

Health care is complicated. They want choices, but it's a narrow set of choices, and we need to figure out not only how to focus in on the right types of choices for individuals that promote value in their own preferences but also make sure everybody has those choices.

I need to underscore the point that you made earlier. We have to have everybody have those choices. It is not fair to have a system where one in three Americans is out of the system at some point in time over 2 years. We have to get everybody in to make sure that this is a high-functioning as well as a fair system.

Mr. DOGGETT. Let me just say, in closing, Mr. Chairman, the suggestion that has been made this morning, not by the witnesses, that we need our health care system to follow the example of the Securities and Exchange Commission and the regulation of the financial market seems to me to be particularly ill-timed, because we have had the idea of government gets out of the way, no regulation of the sub-prime market, and we have a disaster.

I think to follow the notion that we will just turn it over to those that know best and government with get out of the way and Congress won't pay attention or be involved, everything well work out fine—we only need to look at the economic crisis we face today to know that approach does not and will not work.

Chairman SPRATT. Thank you, Mr. Doggett.

Mr. Berry.

Mr. BERRY. Thank you, Mr. Chairman.

Mr. Gratzer, I believe that you in your opening remarks spoke of HSAs and how you thought that was one of the good things that had been done. Do you have information that says how much money they save or do they get better outcomes, why you think that is a better deal?

Dr. GRATZER. Thank you, Mr. Congressman.

We are in the early stages of experimenting with health savings accounts. I think that there have been a plethora of studies that have come out. To really satisfactorily study this issue, we will need far more data over many years.

I think that there is early evidence, certainly some from insurance companies, some from organizations, suggesting that when people are given more financial incentives they do tend to make better decisions. I think we have some early evidence that, and of course we are all very worried about this, people aren't sacrificing care and thus sacrificing their own health in the long run.

As you know, there is one landmark study from the 1970s, one of the largest social science experiments in human history, the RAND Health Insurance Experiment, where a thousand families were put on a free-for-all system, not unlike perhaps what one would get in a country like Canada. A thousand families were put on a user-fee system, and there was no discernible health outcomes except in the poorest of the poor.

So there is evidence that if you separate out smaller items in health care—checkups, X-rays for sprained ankles and so on—from larger items, like, God forbid, one of us is hit by a bus, that people are able to make decisions again. Early evidence from health savings accounts does prove somewhat supportive of this.

Mr. BERRY. Either one of you have a comment?

Ms. LAMBREW. I would just say that I think there are downside risks to this approach, and they are kind of trying it out. One of which is we do have a sense from the research that people are not good at discerning necessary from unnecessary use, so they maybe equally likely to skip the chronic disease medications or the early detection of a disease that does cost as much as other services. So I think there is a risk of losing valuable services as well as wasteful services in the process.

And the second is that, to the extent that people have low income and we're not figuring out a way to address that, we are really creating financial barriers to access to care. And most of the surveys we have seen of these different products are indeed they do increase people's awareness of cost, but they also increase people's self-reported access problems and financial problems associated with those deductibles.

Mr. BERRY. I am curious, as this discussion has taken place, there has been—most of the discussion has been about IT, it seems to me. And I don't discount the value of that. I think we are going to have to do something that improves all that.

I am a little bit surprised that no one has mentioned the value of larger health care pools. I don't believe I have heard it. Maybe it happened when I was out of the room. Or the cost of prescription medicine in, actually, what I consider to be a wacky way that prescription medicine is priced to the American people.

Have you all looked at any of those things as they reflect the cost of health care? And if anybody knows the value of PBMs, I'd like to know what it is, because I have never understood it.

Mr. ORSZAG. Okay, why don't I take a crack at that?

By the way, I should first say I actually have a health savings account myself.

On your former question and the discussion—Mr. Ryan looks surprised by that——

Mr. RYAN. Pleasantly surprised.

Mr. ORSZAG. The discussion we were having before about lack of information about the value of different procedures and what have you, the lack of comparative effectiveness is quite salient because it is often very difficult as a non-medical professional to determine what is or is not valuable.

Let me turn to pharmaceuticals. I think it is they get a lot of attention, but it is important to remember that pharmaceutical spending is about 10 percent of the total health care spending. And that, therefore, there is sort of an inherent limit in some sense to the traction that you get from bending the overall curve through changes in pharmaceutical spending. And in fact there is often some offset in the sense of more pharmaceutical spending may reduce inpatient and other spending.

On pharmaceutical benefit management firms or that technique, we have seen a very dramatic shift towards generics and away from branded drugs, which, by the way, is the primary explanation for why Part D in Medicare is costing a lot less than was projected initially. The shift towards generic drugs that has occurred overall means that overall pharmaceutical spending is much lower than it was projected to be at the time of enactment of Part D. And that has carried through over to Part D, also. So there is no sort of magic to the fact that Part D spending is lower than was projected. That is occurring in drug spending overall, where there has been much less rapid growth than was projected in, say, 2001, 2002, 2003.

Mr. BERRY. Could that savings not have been achieved just by using the pharmacist and his knowledge or her knowledge or by a Medicare-run plan?

Mr. ORSZAG. There are lots of ways of achieving savings.

Again, the question is you need to make sure that the entities that you are hoping will achieve savings have financial incentives to do so. And you mentioned PBMs, they have incentives to achieve those savings.

Ms. LAMBREW. I would like to address your other issue about pools, and I think that was a neglect on my part in my testimony. Because I do think we have heard today the discussion about health care, and it is just not a normal economic good. So the question, if we have price transparency leading to higher collusion on prices, that is not your typical market. So the question becomes, if we do have this different type of system where we have some of this collusion going on, how do we best reduce that? That was a question I think Representative Jordan asked earlier.

And I would argue that trying to have individuals out there shopping for different providers to hopefully lower the price is not a viable option. Having large pools, pool purchasers, sophisticated buyers, insurers trying to figure out how they can, for blocks of people, negotiate down rates, figure out better systems of care, would be more effective, to say nothing of the marketing costs, administrative costs of taking apart our employer-based system today where 60 percent of the people get coverage.

So I would argue that there is fairly significant evidence that if you have large groups of people, not monopolies per se, but large groups of people in purchasing pools that are dealing with a complicated health care system that is fairly consolidated, supply-oriented, you might be able to achieve the kinds of value-oriented health care that we discussed.

Mr. BERRY. Thank you very much.

Dr. GRATZER. I wanted to add, in two or three sentences you have raised some of the biggest issues in health care, obviously going beyond just what we've discussed so far. Pooling is an issue, and the way we buy health insurance right now is very relevant. There are some questions as to whether a 1940s model of employer-based health care is relevant in a day and an age when people are turning over jobs and moving from workplace to workplace. That is a topic for another day.

The other issue, of course, is that prescription drugs often is brought up; and people often get very excited about it. It is only really about 10 percent of overall health spending. It is probably not nearly as fast in growing as a percentage of health spending as, say, hospitals are at this point in time.

It is one area, by the way, where we have seen better information and better pricing availability for people make a difference in that people increasingly choose generics, which probably are more cost-effective for more individuals. That might be one of the very few success stories we can clearly identify, both in Part D and in the private sector.

Chairman SPRATT. Mr. Etheridge.

Mr. ETHERIDGE. Thank you, Mr. Chairman. Thank you for this hearing. I thank our panelists.

I think we all do share the goal of having a health care system that buys high quality and the costs are affordable. We struggle with both those, unfortunately, especially today.

We talk about it—but what we are really talking about is a system last year in the United States we spent about $2.3 trillion, and we are hearing that CBO projections that health care spending will go up to roughly, over the next 75 years, and may increase 10 times. And we're looking at about $28 trillion, which is a number that is so big we can't really comprehend at this point.

Each of you have spoken about the importance of controlling health care costs. Yes, it is what we are about today. How do we do that?

We talked about IT as one of those areas. And just yesterday Congress passed the Medicare Improvement Act, which includes provisions on electronic prescriptions, which I think is a great step forward. I know when I get a prescription from my doctor, his handwriting looks about as bad as mine; and I really wonder how the pharmacist figures it out. But I guess he does so that we get the right kind of medication and the prescription is done, and that is a step in the right direction. Number one, it won't get lost; and, number two, we get the right stuff. So I won't ask you the question on IT because I think we have pretty well beaten that dog to death.

The issue I guess that I do hope you'll cover when I get to the next question is, we have to find a way, I think, in health care how IT can improve our understanding of the system. Because I think, to get the results we want, we really have to understand the problem first—I am not sure we do—that will lead to better care.

And I think consolidation is one of those issues across the country as we look to the charts, hospitals advertise, and if I am sick I want to go to the very best one. I think that is true of everyone else.

You have talked about that through your wife. And that's what happens. We start to do selections. And in the process it is the cost of the increased equipment we buy that we get to.

So I guess the question I want to ask is, one of the curious things about health care is that people don't always have the time, they don't always have the knowledge to wade through all the options. Prime example was the Medicare option as it relates to prescription drugs.

We came out—in North Carolina, I think we had 37 different plans we could go through. Now I have some knowledge of stuff, and my mother-in-law, I was trying to help her, and finally we just decided we weren't going to change. We had an insurance plan. It was so complicated that you had to go to so many different areas to find out whether they covered the drugs she was in.

That is the question. I hope you'll comment on that.

But as we look at the enrollment, people tend to save if they are automatically enrolled and have to opt out. You touched on that earlier. Health care plans, I would be interested in that. Are there ways that we can develop policies that harness this power to improve Medicare or medical efficiencies? Because I think we give too many choices, the first option is not to choose at all, unfortunately, either on the provider or on the consumer side.

Mr. ORSZAG. Yes. Absolutely. And I think this is one of the largest untapped areas of improving health. So, for example, that if you are trying to get someone to get vaccinated next week, saying you should go get vaccinated, you get very low take-up rates. If you say, you should go get vaccinated and here is where you should go and give them a map, higher level. If you automatically make an appointment which they can then cancel, you get extraordinarily higher take-up rates. And, again, you are not imposing anything on anyone because they can always opt out. So you still have the freedom of choice about what happens.

But making it easy for people to do things I think is an extraordinarily powerful thing that we have not tapped across a whole array of policy topics.

And in terms of healthy living, I think what we learn is that if there are even small impediments to exercise or eating well generate very large differences in how much people actually exercise or what they eat. And that is the same story as retirement savings. Just a small impediment, that you have to read through the forms and then sign on the dotted line, that is a big deal in terms of participation rates. We need to be making it easy and simple for people to be eating right and to be exercising, and in the health care system we can be using that same insight.

You mentioned Medicare. In Medicare, for example, one of the things that would pay off, people are always asking me, what can we do that would actually save money in a 5- or 10-year window? E-prescribing actually was scored as saving money.

Another thing that would save money is if we got flu vaccination rates for Medicare beneficiaries up to closer to 100 percent. That would save money in the short run. There is not universal take-up. You could probably get towards universal take-up because most beneficiaries touch a medic or see some Medicare provider during the flu vaccination season. If it were the default that when you went to see a Medicare provider you would receive the flu vaccine unless you opted out—so there are lots of things that you could do.

Ms. LAMBREW. I just would build on it by saying that we also have to figure out ways like that that move beyond the medical system. Because so much of the types of prevention and wellness and behaviors that we need to address are outside of the boundaries of our medical system.

And one study found that if we had a typical physician with 2,500 patients provide the recommended preventative services to that patient group, 7 out of 8 hours of the day would be spent providing prevention. So I do think that part of our challenge in health care is thinking about how we use less costly ways of delivering it in schools, in the workplace. Pharmacists we talked about earlier. Pharmacists see a lot seniors. Why not build pharmacists into these systems to try to ensure immunizations and other good, preventative practices?

So much of prevention is asymptomatic without diagnosis and could be delivered in less costly and more ubiquitous ways, and I think that we need to figure out ways to explore that as well.

Dr. GRATZER. I think we can all agree that one of the easiest ways of saving money is to keep people out of the system in the first place because they are healthy.

Long-term projections always need to be taken with a grain of salt, but people have looked at rising obesity rates in the United States and suggested, between now and 2020, in one study 20 percent of all new costs would be associated with obesity-related illnesses. As you know, that is an entirely avoidable condition. Unfortunately, more and more Americans now qualify as obese. I know the last statistical analysis suggested that maybe we had plateaued out, something like one in five Americans qualify as obese; 40 percent are overweight.

I think, though, when we look at public health—and this is an area of extraordinary interest to me—we have to be a little bit cautious. Life isn't as easy as it was in the 1960s. As you know, in the early 1960s, before the greatest public health revolution of the 20th century, two-thirds of Americans actually thought there was no connection between tobacco use and cancer. Because of the Surgeon General's report and because of the government's efforts on educating, by the end of the 1960s the vast majority of people saw that obvious connection.

Today, people are actually extremely informed. There was a study recently done by an economist suggesting that tobacco users, cigarette smokers in fact tended to overestimate the risk to their health.

So it is one thing to say, look, prevention is good. We have to deal with prevention, though, through the challenges of our time, which are that people are more educated than ever before and more informed on health issues more than before.

Why is it that they continue to make bad decisions? Well, there are economic factors. There are cultural factors.

But that is equally relevant I think to these discussions. How can we save money with health care over the long term? Have more healthy Americans.

Mr. ORSZAG. Can I just add one more really quick comment, which is that we are seeing—smoking is a good example where the reductions in smoking rates that occurred disproportionately occurred among higher-income, better-educated people and did not occur to the same degree at the bottom of the socioeconomic distribution.

One of the consequences relative to that kind of change is that we are seeing literally an explosion in life expectancy inequality, where life expectancy is going up on average, but it is going up way faster at the top of the socioeconomic distribution, and it is flat or by some measures may even be declining slightly at the bottom.

One of the things that may be the consequence of changing defaults and changing social norms and what have you is to kind of retilt that a little bit. That is what happens in retirement savings. What happens when you make retirement saving automatic is that you get low- and moderate-income workers participating at rates that are close to those for higher-income workers which no other policy intervention seems to be able to accomplish.

Mr. ETHERIDGE. Thank you, Mr. Chairman. I yield back.

Chairman SPRATT. Mr. Moore.

Mr. MOORE of Kansas. Thank you, Mr. Chairman; and thanks to the three panelists for being here.

Dr. Orszag, you emphasized in your opening statement that our health care system's use of electronic medical records would be of benefit, I think—establishing a system. As I provided you a copy of the Dear Colleague letter that Mr. Ryan and I have circulated to our colleagues in support of such a system. And I understand and I appreciate your comment back, and we will review the study that you mentioned there and certainly correct it if it needs correcting as far as the information.

But we have introduced the Independent Health Record Trust Act, which would establish a modern, market-driven, nationwide health information technology network by providing for the creation of nonprofit health record trusts in this country. Under this system, persons would have—the individuals would have the option of signing up for an account to be managed by a health record trust similar to the way banks offer to maintain credit card accounts.

Right now, patients walk into a hospital or a physician's office and the first thing they are handed is a history form to be completed and provide information about medical history. Sometimes the patients get it right, and sometimes they don't.

And I think I read into what—at least what I heard you say Dr. Orszag, that we could benefit from these miraculous little devices called computers now and bring maybe the health care delivery system into the 21st century.

I am not trying to be facetious here, but I am just saying I think there is a lot of opportunities for errors when patients are asked every time they check into a medical facility or a doctor's office to complete this patient history form. And, again, they may or may not have the correct information, and the information could be compiled and could be distributed with the authority of the patient.

My wife is a practicing nurse for more than 20 years, and she says patient confidentiality and protecting patient's information is very important. And we certainly understand that and agree with that as well. In fact, she says a woman who goes in for a skin condition to a dermatologist, the dermatologist probably, probably does not need to see her OB/GYN records, and she should have the authority to make that decision.

But our point is that—and I would like you and the other panelists, if you have thoughts about this, to comment on how much benefit we could derive—our country could derive and especially our people could benefit from the establishment of this kind of system. Because, again, we want to get it right, but we want to provide information to the caregivers with the authority of the patients.

A CBO study of health information technology released in May laid out some of the improvements in efficiency that can be captured through health information technology, but the analysis, in my opinion, seemed to downplay some of the health and safety benefits of the health information technology and that the full value of adoption of such a system can only be realized through the system-wide change like we proposed here.

And I guess I just—do you think the widespread, integrated implementation of a national health information network, particularly one that protects the privacy and security of an individual's records, is a critical component of any effort to control the growth of health care costs and improve the efficiency and effectiveness of our system?

And the last thing I want to ask—and will stop and you can talk—is somebody—I think it was you, Dr. Orszag, but whomever—mentioned the Veterans Administration system; and I've heard from many people that they have a pretty good system overall. And I guess I would like you just to give any additional comments you might have there.

Because we've just got to get this right. It just seems like we are not delivering the best health care to people if the physicians and the people who are providing the treatment and the hospitals don't have all the correct information they need. Again, with these devices, that should be kind of something that shouldn't require a lot of thought.

Thank you.

Mr. ORSZAG. Sure, let me just first say health information technology in my view is necessary but not sufficient. So it is critical to improving the efficiency of the health system, but by itself, if that's all you did, it wouldn't be sufficient to capture the $700 billion opportunity that we were discussing before.

The VA system, through its Vista health IT system, does have one model. And we actually came out with a preliminary report.

We are going to have a fuller report on the VA system and what we can learn from it out I think later this year.

You have to remember that that system basically is contained. It's not a fully integrated system, but it is closer than the rest of the health system to the sort of full array of things of what you would want. There are incentives for higher-value care. The information is processed in terms of what is coming out. It's not just the health IT systems. It is a health IT system in a structure that makes sense.

The analogy that Laura Adams, who runs the Rhode Island Quality Institute uses, is: getting more efficiency out of the health system is like waiting for toast to come out of the toaster. And some people say we need to plug the toaster in. That is like health IT. Other people say we have to go to the store and we have to buy the bread. And other people say you have to put the bread in the hole and press the lever down and wait for it to come back up. You need to do all of those things, obviously; and just plugging the toaster in by itself is not going to get the bread to come out. And that is my point.

Mr. MOORE of Kansas. Thank you very much.

Any other comments?

Thank you.

Chairman SPRATT. Ms. Kaptur.

Ms. KAPTUR. Thank you, Mr. Chairman, very much; and, again, thank our long-suffering panelists here for being with us and for the great work that you do.

I wanted to ask, Dr. Orszag, in your testimony on page 3 you have included a map and it is entitled, Medicare Spending per Beneficiary in the United States, by Hospital Referral Region. I would be very interested and I am sure all the members would be in our own regions, since these maps don't reflect congressional districts and what that might say about our respective regions.

Are those dollar amounts merely a reflection that we have more elderly or is it the system that is operating in the area and the way it expends dollars? And if so, if it is the second, then could you comment on the areas that are in the top category and what those higher costs might reflect?

Mr. ORSZAG. Yes. Most of that variation is occurring because of the intensity with which Medicare beneficiaries are treated. In those areas that are at the top of the cost curve that are darker in this map, there is a lot more stuff that happens to you.

So if you get sick, you are much more likely to be hospitalized—for any given condition, you are much more likely to be hospitalized. You are much more likely to spend a lot more time in the hospital. You are much more likely to see lots of specialists. You are much more likely to have lots of tests done to you. And when there is ambiguity about what should happen, you're much more likely to have an expensive procedure undertaken.

So the more intense service is provided. But the kicker is it doesn't look like that greater intensity actually buys you anything in terms of better health outcomes.

Ms. KAPTUR. That is what I want to know. One of the sentences that you have in your testimony is some of the highest cost areas are concentrated around the top U.S. medical centers. Now that is very interesting.

One of the issues that we face in our region is the ability to keep attracting good doctors and research-related doctors, because they go off to where these medical centers are where they can do more intensive research and where there is a broader array of physicians. And I see—just as with airline deregulation and you have these mammoth, big airports in certain places, I see what is happening in our health care system, these mammoth health systems that are creating, rearranging the way we have doctors arrayed in this country, for example, and it is a great concern. I was wondering what that map is really telling us.

Well, let me ask this question. Do you see any correlation, Dr. Orszag, in work that you have done between the cost of medical care and pharmaceuticals? And one of my big questions there is, when a pharmaceutical comes off patent, are there studies that show that prices go down?

Mr. ORSZAG. Yes.

Ms. KAPTUR. Is it by drug?

Mr. ORSZAG. What you see is—the patterns around when something—a brand new drug goes off patent are actually often quite interesting, but let me actually—we can raise—there is legislation, for example, for so-called follow-on biologics which would create a pathway for FDA approval of complex molecules, complex drugs, not simple molecular drugs but complex molecular drugs to get FDA approval.

We have scored savings to that legislation because having that follow-on biologic, which is sort of a generic type thing, enter the market would help, once a brand-new drug came off patent, drive down the price. I mean, basically, the mechanism is, once something is off patent and generics are a more prominent part of the market, there is price pressure on the old, branded drug, but then consumers are shifting towards this generics——

Ms. KAPTUR. You can't watch television without seeing 15 ads in an hour. I mean, if you weren't sick before you started watching, you will be sick after. So the amount of money it takes to do that across this country, unbelievable.

I am interested in pharmaceuticals and the rising cost of health care in this country. Any studies, any information you have would be most interesting, especially when most of those pharmaceuticals are made offshore.

Let me give you an example. Heparin—not a new drug. I don't know what the prices of heparin are. I would be interested if there is a study that tells me. But we had lots of people die in this country taking heparin that was manufactured in China.

I would like to know, if you can tell me, what it would cost to manufacture that right here in this country? What is the cost advantage to the company to manufacture in China?

And we have people in my district that died taking that in full faith that it was examined and so forth. How can that happen? It is a formula that is well-known. It is a very old drug. I don't know how much it costs. What should it cost? And what happened that we can't make that in this country? Is it a complicated formula? And, if it is, maybe we should be making it here. Can you comment on the heparin situation and how that could have possibly have happened in the year 2008 in this country?

Mr. ORSZAG. I am going to stay away from talking about a specific drug, but let me come back to your broader question. There is no question that pharmaceuticals play some role in rising health care costs. But I do think it is important to remember they seem to receive an amount of attention that is disproportionate to their role either in cost growth or in cost. They are about 10 percent of total health care spending.

Most of that $700 billion inefficiency that I was mentioning before occurs because of variations in—that we were talking about in this map—occurs because of variations in hospitalizations and surgery rates and MRIs and other imaging and what have you. So pharmaceuticals are part of the puzzle, but relative to their actual contribution they receive way more media and policy attention than their sort of numerical contribution would suggest.

Ms. KAPTUR. Well, I know my time is up, Mr. Chairman. But I would be very interested in, Dr. Orszag, on the map if you could take the 9th Congressional District of Ohio and tell me—because you can't really tell where it is on here—if you could go down to that level and tell me what those numbers mean for us. What does that translate into our particular region—I am sure other members on the committee would be similarly interested.

And then, on the pharmaceutical issue, I would be very interested in anybody on the panel, if you know where I would find this, I would like to know the cost accounting of manufacture of heparin. I would like to know how much it costs, I would like to know where it is manufactured, and I'd like to know what it would take to manufacture it in this country.

Incidentally, all the heparin cases are being referred to a Federal court in my district, so I have a really special interest in this.

What are the economics of driving that production offshore? I don't know if you have access to studies on that or if you could refer me somewhere, but I am very, very—because that is not the only one. That is one I am really paying close attention to.

Why can't we make that here? What are the economics that are driving that offshore? And then I want to know what it costs if you go off and you buy it through Medicare, let's say. You must have access to data. Do any of you feel comfortable in referring me to sources on that?

Ms. LAMBREW. I will say one of the interesting experiences that I had in the '90s when I worked in the Clinton administration was we were all debating the Medicare drug benefit at that point and looked into how do we understand the relative prices of a set of a basket of drugs. And it is very difficult to try to go in and try to look at who pays what from wholesale price to retail price to Medicaid price to the cost of manufacturing. And we found our study concluded that we don't have the systems in place to know.

So I think it is a very hard question that you have asked. I am not sure there is information on that.

I would put in a plug for trying to ensure at least that the data support agencies that you have—CBO, GAO, CRS—get access to some of the drug data that we are getting through Medicare. I mean, Medicare is now a major payer for prescription drugs in the

United States of America. Yet we—you all in government don't necessarily have the types of scrutiny of the data that we are getting to figure out what is working, what is not working and what are the costs of the different drugs. So I think that there is some improved information sharing that could happen with the new Medicare drug benefit to begin to feed into a larger system to help answer some of these questions.

Ms. KAPTUR. Thank you.

Thank you, Mr. Chairman.

Chairman SPRATT. Just two questions and then Mr. Ryan has a question to close.

Going back to this variegated map of the United States and costs per capita. Dr. Orszag, you said it can't adequately be explained. I understand we are trying to discern the reasons for these different patterns of expenditure. But, number one, what can we do to better discern and speed up the effort to determine what is at the root cause of these differences in per capita costs?

And, secondly, how do we disseminate that information? How do we institutionalize it and disseminate it? Would it be worthwhile to consider the creation of an institute at NIH for the delivery of health care in order to develop information in a package form that can be systematically disseminated amongst physicians, practitioners all over the country?

Mr. ORSZAG. Let me answer that in two stages.

First, with regard to the regional variation, CBO came out with a report a couple months ago looking at what is known. There is ongoing work about getting at the cause. There is a group up at Dartmouth, the Wennberg Center, that is exclusively devoted to this kind of regional analysis.

And CBO is currently expending a lot of internal resources, putting together two significant volumes that will be out at the end of this year to present policymakers and others with options for improving the efficiency of the health care system, among which will be options to try to get at this regional variation.

The second part of your question had to do with ways of disseminating information, and I think we have touched upon a Federal health board idea. There are related ideas about some comparative effectiveness entity or entities beyond the existing AHRQ that is part of HHS.

It is crucial to—coming back to the basic point, just having information floating out there is not going to do the trick. In order for information to matter, it has to affect the way medicine is practiced. And in order to affect the way medicine is practiced, you need to be getting the information especially to medical professionals and doctors. And then you need to be giving them incentives to, again, move towards better care.

So I do think there are institutional gaps in our ability to do both of those things right now, and that is why there are discussions about whether some change in institutional forms would be beneficial.

Chairman SPRATT. Thank you.

Mr. Ryan.

Mr. RYAN. I will follow up on that.

I guess at the end of the day the different approaches we may look at come from sort of a bottom-up market-based approach or sort a of top-down government-based approach. But I think we are all coming to consensus on the need on some of the design features, and then we will squabble over a few other details. But this is a productive debate going in the right direction, nonetheless.

Dr. Orszag, you said something when I stepped out which was interesting. Unless you change the payment system, you are never going to have a more efficient health care system. Obviously, I think that is totally accurate.

Let me ask you this. The trustees of Medicare are telling us we have a $34 trillion unfunded present value liability with respect to Medicare. Can you change the payment system without spending more money? And can you change the payment system that actually saves more money? And, if so, can you quantify that?

Mr. ORSZAG. There is no question that—first of all, I will try to avoid only saying interesting things when you are not here. But there is no——

Mr. RYAN. The HSA comment was the most interesting.

Mr. ORSZAG. There is no question that you could save money through payment methodology changes within Medicare today——

Mr. RYAN. Net.

Mr. ORSZAG. Net. That is not hard. Because, you know, simplistically, you could ratchet payments down.

The key question is, can you change the payment methodology in a way that not only saves money but is sustainable over time and that changes the way medicine is practiced so that you are bending the curve not only for Medicare but for the health system as a whole? Because, if not, you are just going to create the kind of issue that we have with the sustainable growth rate formula and other artificial constraints that operate just on Medicare. If you are not affecting the overall rate of health care spending over time, all you would create with ratcheting down Medicare reimbursement rates is an access problem.

Mr. RYAN. That is basically why I asked the question.

If anybody else wants a stab at that, please have at it.

Ms. LAMBREW. You also asked the question of can you save without spending. I think the question depends, can you get these types of bending-the-curve systems without an up-front investment. And I would argue that we do need to consider investing in health information technology, investing in the research to undergird this system, getting people into insurance arrangements so that they have the same choices and benefits that we all have.

I could make a case—and I will just say one more thing. Of that $700 billion that Dr. Orszag has suggested is out there, remember that is not all public. A good proportion of that is private savings. Trying to figure out how we capture and redirect in a system is hard to do at the Federal level.

Mr. RYAN. Do these investment costs have to be borne by the taxpayer or could they be borne by the market?

Ms. LAMBREW. I would make a case that if the goal is to figure out where the Federal Government invests in public goods, then I would argue HIT and comparative effectiveness are public goods. I would argue trying to help low-income people afford health insurance is not something the markets can do. I think there needs to be an up-front Federal investment.

I can make a case that that up-front Federal investment should and potentially could yield systemic, if not Federal, savings within a budget window. And that is our challenge, is to figure out how academics and policymakers can come together to say, let's invest now but ensure that that investment yields long-run savings. That is our challenge.

Mr. RYAN. Yeah, and scoring it.

Ms. LAMBREW. That's his challenge.

Chairman SPRATT. Could I add one final question?

If we want to disseminate the information and have this diffusion of knowledge on a more equal basis and have information technology, latest technology, wouldn't it make sense for the government simply to develop this software, this program and maybe develop it on an open source basis so that it is changed, upgraded from time to time? It would mean that everybody was operating with the same system.

Mr. ORSZAG. Well, the Federal Government has sort of tried that in the sense of almost basically giving away a health IT system.

I think it may turn out to be more productive for the Federal Government to set certain standards regarding interoperability and privacy and then let the market develop for the specific systems that can fulfill those standards, that the history of government innovation in technology is not marked by substantial successes. So the approach of kind of saying, here is what we need the system to do.

And, again, coming back to our earlier discussion, if your system doesn't do that, you are not going to get paid under Medicare, may wind up being the most auspicious approach.

Chairman SPRATT. Well, I think one of your studies noted part of the problem is there are still a lot of small-sized practices, and these practices find it difficult to spread the cost of expensive software over the relatively small volumes of businesses that they do. If the government was bearing much of the cost of development of the software like this, you would be able to have these smaller firms take advantage of it.

Mr. ORSZAG. Yeah. But the problem is it is often not just the purchase of the software that is the cost, it is that you are disrupting your operations for some period of time while people learn how to use it. And all the other sort of process changes that are involved. So just even giving away software will not get you universal take-up among small practitioners.

Mr. RYAN. I think, if you take a look at the market, you have five or six basic big players doing the software systems out there. A couple of them are from Wisconsin, GE and Epic. And if the government simply requires interoperability, it patches on these programs so that they can talk to each other, that in and of itself is a step in the right direction. But the market continually innovates, continually competes and meets the needs without the government designing the software systems because you already have private firms doing the design.

The question is, are they going to be done in the stovepipe fashion that they are today or will the government be a flattener so that these things can talk to each other and then the market can continue to innovate and provide these benefits? That is where I think we can make a difference. That is what Dennis and I are trying to achieve in our bill, among some other things.

Chairman SPRATT. Let me thank all three of our witnesses for coming today, for your presentations. We very much appreciate it, and we think we will probably revisit this topic from time to time in the future. Thank you very much for your participation today.

[Whereupon, at 12:07 p.m., the committee was adjourned.]

○